WEEKEND MAKES

PUNCH NEEDLE

25 QUICK AND EASY PROJECTS TO MAKE

WEEKEND MAKES

PUNCH NEEDLE

25 QUICK AND EASY PROJECTS TO MAKE

SARA MOORE

First published 2020 by
Guild of Master Craftsman Publications Ltd Castle Place,
166 High Street, Lewes,
East Sussex, BN7 1XU

Text © Sara Moore, 2020
Copyright in the Work © GMC Publications Ltd, 2020

ISBN 978-1-78494-589-3

Senior Project Editor: Kandy Regis
Managing Art Editor: Darren Brant
Art Editor: Jacqui Crawford
Photography: Sara Moore & Quail Studio

Colour origination by GMC Reprographics
Printed and bound in China

CONTENTS

Introduction 7

TOOLS AND MATERIALS 8
Punch Needles 8
Fabric 9
Frames and Hoops 10
Yarn 11

BASIC EQUIPMENT 12
GETTING STARTED 14
Preparing the Fabric 14
Drawing a Straight Line 14
Tracing a Pattern 14
Stretching the Fabric 15
Using the Punch Needle 16
Different Stitches 19
Tidying Up 21
Tips and Tricks 21

FINISHING TECHNIQUES 23
Steaming 23
Gluing 23
Hemming 24
Whipping 25

PROJECTS
Small Geometric Cushion Cover 26
Large Geometric Cushion Cover 30
Handbag 34

Tool Tub 38
Large Storage Tub 42
Geometric Wall Art 46
Pin Cushion 50
Small Plant Pot Cover 54
Large Plant Pot Cover 58
Doorstop 62
Pendant Wall Hanging 66
Hanging Heart Decoration 70
Coasters 74
Trivet 78
Napkin Holders 82
Bookmark 86
Celestial Hoop Art 90
Tablet Cover 94
Card Holder 98
Sunglasses Case 102
Passport Cover 106
Clutch Bag 110
Laptop Pouch 114
Upcycled Cushion Cover 118
Abstract Wall Hanging 122

Templates 126
Resources 142
Acknowledgements 142
Index 143

INTRODUCTION

Welcome to *Weekend Makes – Punch Needle*, a fabulous book featuring 25 modern abstract design projects for yourself, your home or to give as gifts.

Whether you're looking for a new skill to try or you've tried punch needle already and are looking for a new project to take you up to another level, then there's plenty here to tempt you. Some are super quick and can be completed in just an hour or so, while others will take a little longer depending on your ability. Each of the projects is graded as 'Easy' or 'Moving On'. Basic craft skills are all you need for the really simple 'Easy' projects, which are suitable for beginners. Whilst the 'Moving On' items are slightly bigger projects that just require a little more making up and finishing skills and will take a little longer to make.

The craft of punch needle is related to the more traditional craft of rug hooking, the key difference being that rug hooking works from the top of the fabric to pull loops up, whereas punch needle uses a tool to push loops down through the fabric. Unlike most crafts, punch needle is a simple technique that requires little dexterity and can easily be learnt by all. It has a relaxing rhythm and speed once you have mastered the skill, which makes it a really satisfying technique. There is a range of projects in this book including accessories, wall decorations, cushions, storage and tableware to suit beginners through to those looking for more of a challenge.

A section on the basic punch needle techniques can be found at the front of the book, along with step-by-step photos. This details all the essentials you need to know from tools and materials, fabric preparation, design placement and using the punch needle to stitching and finishing techniques. I suggest you take time to read this before you start any of the projects.

Once you become more experienced with the craft of punch needle you can raid your workbasket and try experimenting with all sorts, like strips of jersey fabric, torn-up bed sheets and string. Create textured items out of fabric and yarn and add embellishments to almost any item to give a personalised look.

For this collection of projects I've worked in wool and used my signature palette of chalky shades to create a modern, contemporary feel in soft muted tones. The really great thing is that all the projects would work equally well in a brighter palette of punchy colours if this is more your thing. Each of my patterns includes clear instructions and finishing techniques, as well as a few tips.

The 25 projects in this book are stylish but also practical for everyday use. I have had so much fun making these and I really hope you enjoy making them too.

Sara Moore

TOOLS AND MATERIALS

There are a few core components required for punch needle rug hooking. You need a punch needle, base fabric, something to stretch your fabric on to (frame or hoop) and yarn.

PUNCH NEEDLES

There are a number of different punch needles available and they can be separated into two categories:

- Yarn punch needles
- Embroidery floss punch needles

In this book we will be using punch needles for yarn. Punch needles may look similar on occasion, but the punch needles that take yarn will have a wider needle to accommodate the thicker fibre.

All the projects in this book are completed using Oxford punch needles. Oxford punch needles are designed by punch needle expert Amy Oxford. They are ergonomically designed for comfort and speed, and are an excellent choice of punch needle. They come in two widths: regular and fine. The regular needles use thick, chunky or bulky yarn, whereas the fine needles use aran or worsted-weight yarn. Within the different widths there are different options for loop heights: each needle creates a different loop height, which is denoted by a number. In this book we will be using the following needles:

- Oxford #10 regular punch needle (creates ¼in (6cm) loop)
- Oxford #14 fine punch needle (creates ⅛in (3cm) loop

FABRIC

When you use a punch needle, you need a base fabric to punch into. The base fabric you use with your punch needle needs to be strong in order to withstand the constant pressure from your punching. The most common base fabric is called monk's cloth. Monk's cloth is a loose, even-weave cotton fabric, which is specifically designed for punch needle. The loose, equally spaced holes are wide enough to allow the punch needle through, yet tight enough to hold the loops in place. Monk's cloth has a double thread running through it, which makes it very hard-wearing.

One of the best properties of this hard-wearing fabric is that you can 'frog' your work. To frog your work means you can pull it out and do it again. This makes the fabric very forgiving and great for beginners! I always encourage students to have a go at pulling out stitches and re-punching. It can be very satisfying. The monk's cloth used for these projects has white 2in guidelines running through the fabric. These are very useful for ensuring your design is straight when stretching it on a frame or hoop. Monk's cloth will often be listed as having a certain number of threads or holes per inch. The monk's cloth used for these projects has 24-26 threads per inch, also referred to as 12-13 holes per inch.

You can dye your monk's cloth, which is great if you want to leave some of the background fabric exposed.

Once you become familiar with the properties of monk's cloth you can look for similar fabrics to work on, however if you are making a rug or another project expected to take a good deal of wear and tear, you would be best to use a fabric designed for punch needle.

FRAMES AND HOOPS

A frame or hoop is required to stretch your base fabric on to and hold it taut whilst you are working. The tighter you can stretch your fabric the better. A tight base fabric will make punching easier and not too taxing on your hands. A loose, saggy fabric will make for uneven stitches and put unwanted strain on your hands and wrists.

There are a few different frame / hoop options:

- Wooden stretcher bars
- Carpet tack frame
- Gripper strip frame
- No-slip hoop
- Embroidery hoop

WOODEN STRETCHER BARS

You can buy wooden canvas stretcher bars in multiple sizes. These make for an easy, affordable frame. Once assembled you can stretch your fabric over the frame and use staples or drawing pins to secure. This doesn't always keep your fabric taut and it can sag during punching, but you can easily re-tighten the fabric as you punch using the drawing pins or staples. It's also easy to remove your piece afterwards.

CARPET TACK FRAME

Carpet tacks can be bought in strips from most hardware stores. Using a wooden frame as a base, the carpet tacks can be attached to the frame creating an affordable and effective punch needle frame. The tacks are very sharp, so after stretching your fabric you will need to cover the protruding tacks – rolled up felt works great for this. Although the tacks are sharp and appear that they would shred the fabric, if using with monk's cloth the fabric is strong enough to endure the tacks.

GRIPPER STRIP FRAME

Gripper strips are rubber strips filled with small, staple-like teeth, which grip the backing fabric in place, like Velcro. Gripper strips can be used on frames for both punch needle and traditional rug hooking. The strips grip the fabric allowing the pattern to be repositioned as you go. The strips can be attached to a wooden frame of any size.

The size of your punch needle will dictate the thickness of yarn you should use. As a rule of thumb, the regular Oxford punch needles use thick, chunky or bulky yarns, with the fine needles using aran or worsted-weight. This book uses standard yarn weight groups set by the Craft Yarn Council (craftyarncouncil.com).

If your yarn is too thin for the needle you want to use and you find it slips, try doubling or tripling up the strands in your needle. If you have a yarn which is particularly slippery (like silk or some cottons), you can thread this through the needle with a more coarse yarn and then it should work.

NO-SLIP HOOPS

Morgan 'no-slip' hoops are hardy, plastic hoops which have a patented tongue and groove feature. When fabric is placed between the outer and inner rings, the tongue and groove locks it in place, keeping the fabric taut. The hoops come in multiple sizes in increments of an inch.

If you are making a rug or another object that is required to be hard-wearing, it is advisable to use rug yarn. Rug yarn is generally more coarse and less refined than a knitting or crochet yarn and therefore is tough enough to be walked on!

EMBROIDERY HOOP

If you put your fabric into a standard wooden embroidery hoop, you will be able to make the first few punches before the fabric starts to sag. If you would like to punch directly into an embroidery hoop as you wish to use the hoop to frame the piece afterwards, you can glue the fabric in place to keep it taut (for more information see page 22).

Punch needle is great for using up odds and ends of yarn. If you're making a smaller project, the quantities of yarn required will be quite small (a little goes a long way when punching). Consider using up some scraps, which will make your project sustainable too!

YARN

As a rule you want your yarn to move smoothly through the needle. Any yarn that is too fluffy or lumpy is likely to get stuck or snag in the needle. It is better to choose a smoother yarn when you are learning to prevent this causing a problem.

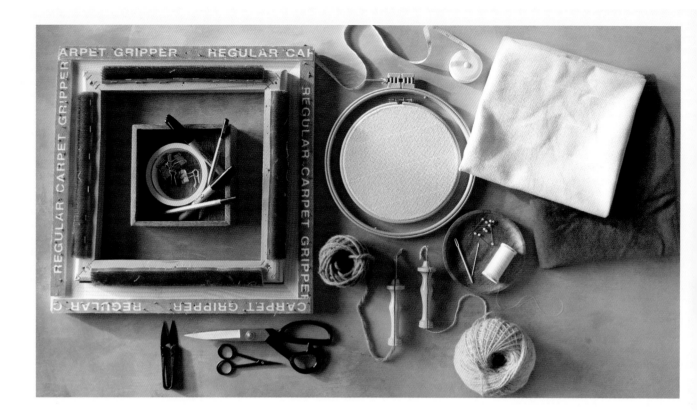

BASIC
EQUIPMENT

Masking tape: This works well for taping over the edges of the fabric to stop them from fraying. If you would rather (and have the option) you can use an overlocker to serge the edges, or a small zigzag stitch on a sewing machine.

Marker pens and pencil: Marker pens are useful for tracing your design on to the fabric. It can be a little unnerving using such a permanent pen to draw straight on to your fabric, but don't worry, you'll be completely covering it in stitches so it won't show through. A pencil is perfect for drawing a straight line on your fabric (see page 14 for more information on drawing a straight line).

Paper: Tracing paper works really well for tracing the designs from the book. If you have squared paper this can be another option.

Tape measure: To measure out your fabric for cutting. It is also useful to have one to hand when deciding where to place your design on the fabric and ensuring you have left the required border size around your design.

Scissors: A decent, sharp pair of dressmaking or fabric scissors is essential for cutting your base fabric and any finishing fabrics. For cutting the ends of your yarn it is useful to have a small, pointed pair of embroidery scissors, or alternatively you can use a pair of thread snips. However, the embroidery scissors double up as a good 'poking' tool for moving loops into place.

Pins: Quilting pins are great for pinning hems or attaching backing fabric to your punched piece. The larger, bobble pin head is useful as the base fabric has holes in; pins without something on the end may slip through the fabric.

Needles: Hand-sewing needles are used for hemming or stitching projects together. Larger darning needles are used for whip-stitching the edges of a punched piece with yarn.

Clips: Clips, pegs or binder or foldback clips are useful for keeping a rolled edge in place, ready to be whip-stitched.

Thread: A neutral thread (similar to your base fabric) is required for hemming your finished pieces. For stitching that shows, it is optimal to have a colour that complements your finishing fabric.

Iron, ironing board and hand towel: For pieces that require steaming before finishing, you will need an iron, ironing board and a hand towel. Hand towels work better than a tea towel or dishcloth. It is also handy to have a bowl of cold water or a tap nearby.

GETTING STARTED

PREPARING THE FABRIC

All of the projects in this book (apart from the upcycled cushion) use monk's cloth as the base fabric. Once you have cut the required size of fabric for your project, you will note that the edges fray. In order to prevent this becoming worse you need to protect the edges. If you have an overlocker or serger, or a sewing machine, you can run a line of stitching along the edge to secure. A quick and easy method if you do not have one of these is to use masking tape (1).

DRAWING A STRAIGHT LINE

Some of the patterns are easy to trace once you have your outline in place. If your outline is a square or rectangle, here is a little trick to help you get a straight line. You will see on the monk's cloth that there are slight dips in between the rows of threads, almost like a channel. If you press a pencil down firmly, and drag it through one of these channels, it will give you a perfectly straight line (2).

TRACING A PATTERN

When tracing a pattern from a book, it is easier if you first trace the design on to a piece of paper (tracing paper works best, but alternatively plain or squared A4 paper will also work). With the design now on a separate piece of paper you can trace the image on to the base fabric. If you have a lightbox this is easy enough to do, but alternatively a window also works. Place the paper behind the monk's cloth and trace on to the fabric using a marker pen.

Don't worry if you make any mistakes, as you'll be covering the fabric in stitches so you won't see the marks.

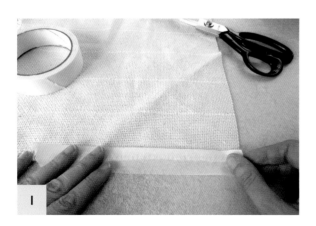

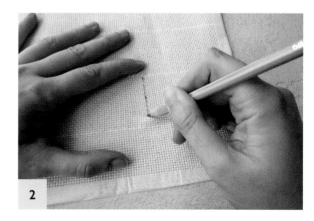

STRETCHING THE FABRIC

Once you have transferred your design on to the fabric you need to stretch your fabric as tight as possible on to whichever frame or hoop you are using (see tools and materials – frames and hoops, for further information on which one to use). With all methods, the aim is not to distort the shape of your design. Use the white guidelines on the fabric to ensure your design does not warp.

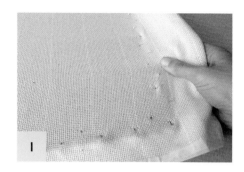

Carpet tack frame: Take care when stretching fabric on to a carpet tack frame as the tacks are very sharp. Lay the fabric over the frame so that the design is in the middle. Holding opposite sides of the fabric, pull gently over the tacks, slowly tightening the fabric **(1)**.

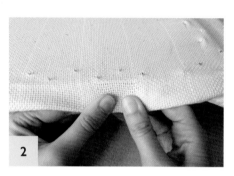

Repeat on the other sides. Using both hands, lift small sections of fabric up and over the tacks, all the way around the frame until all of the fabric is as tight as a drum **(2)**.

Once your base fabric is really tight, cover the exposed tacks with some rolled up fabric. You can secure this using scraps of yarn tied around the frame and fabric **(3)**.

Gripper strip frame: Lay the fabric over the top of the gripper frame and centre your design. Gently pull opposite sides of the fabric over the strips until your fabric is tight. The strips will grip the fabric like Velcro. You can easily release the fabric when you have finished punching by pulling up the edges.

No-slip hoop: Loosen the screw and separate the outer and inner rings to expose the tongue and groove feature **(4)**.

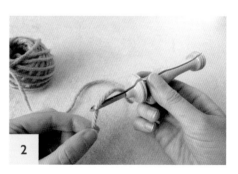

Lay the inner ring on a surface and put the fabric on top, now place the outer ring over. Tighten the screw and then use both hands to get the fabric as taut as possible in the hoop. It's often easier to tighten the screw a little, then the fabric, then back to the screw, until your fabric is super tight **(5)**.

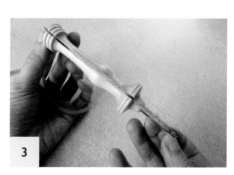

USING THE PUNCH NEEDLE

The punch needle works by pushing a piece of yarn through fabric, which when pulled upwards forms a small loop. The base fabric has small, evenly placed holes, which grip the loops. The density of the loops keeps the yarn in place, meaning there is no need for knots or glue!

The Oxford punch needles are ergonomically designed and comfortable to punch with for sustained periods of time. They do not require a threader, which means you can change your yarns easily. You can buy Oxford punch needles either boxed, or unboxed. If you buy a boxed Oxford punch needle it comes with a handy guide and stitch gauge, which is well worth the few extra pounds and will go over much of what is covered here **(1)**.

A punch needle can be held in either hand, great if you're lucky enough to be ambidextrous, and also perfect for those of us with one dominant hand, whichever that may be. The punch needle has a smooth wooden handle, with a short metal needle protruding from it. There is a continuous channel / slit that runs the length of the handle and needle. On one side of the needle there is a small eye / hole.

Threading the needle: Unwind your ball of yarn and make sure there is plenty of slack on it. Hold the needle so that the channel is facing upwards. Take the tail end of your yarn and push the end through the eye of the needle, pull it through **(2)**.

Rest the yarn along the channel of the needle **(3)**. Pull the yarn through the channel by alternating pulling the tail and ball ends of the yarn. A few pulls each way and you should feel it 'pop' into the handle **(4)**. Your needle is now threaded!

If you are using a 'fine' Oxford needle there is an extra step of putting the yarn through the small guiding hoop before putting it in the eye **(5)**.

When I punch I find it easiest to hold the frame or hoop in my non-dominant hand, allowing it to rest on the edge of a table to steady it. After a little while you will find what is comfortable for you.

Starting to punch: Hold the needle in your dominant hand, as you would hold a pen or pencil; ensure that the channel is facing you. With the needle at a slight angle to the fabric, push the needle in, all the way down so the fabric touches the wooden handle **(6)**. Pull your needle up slowly so that the tip is just exposed above the fabric. Keeping the needle close to the fabric, move the needle forward a little (approximately 2-3 holes) and push back down again **(7)**.

You want the needle to feel almost as if it is dragging across the fabric before pushing back down again. If you pull your needle up too high, your stitches will not stay in and be uneven in loop height. By pushing the needle fully into the fabric each time, down to the wooden handle, you will ensure an even loop height on the other side. Punch slowly and smoothly and you will soon find a rhythm.

When you are punching, ensure the channel faces in the direction you are moving your needle. If I am punching upwards, away from my body in a straight line, the channel should be following the line I am punching **(8)**.

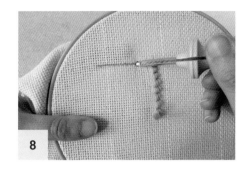

Finishing a row of stitching: When you come to the end of the row you are punching, pull your needle up out of the fabric slowly, so that a small amount of yarn is visible, approximately ⅜in (1cm). Pinch this yarn between your fingers and snip off close to the fabric **(9)**.

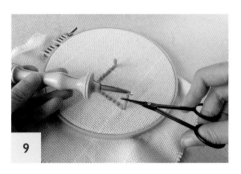

Use the closed end of your embroidery scissors and push this end back through the hole it came out of so it is now on the same side as the loops **(10)**.

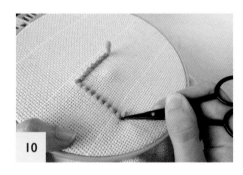

Turning corners: When turning corners in your design, ensure your needle is fully inserted into the fabric. When your needle is fully inserted, you can then either turn the hoop or frame you are working on, or turn the needle, it is personal preference and you may find that you do one naturally. Either way, turn and ensure that when turned the channel of your needle is still facing in the direction you are punching.

Tips to remember

Always have the needle facing in the direction you are punching.

Fully insert the punch needle into the fabric, down to the wooden handle, for even-sized loops.

Have lots of slack on the ball of yarn, allowing it to move smoothly through the needle.

DIFFERENT STITCHES

When you use a punch needle, the side that you are working on will have a flat stitch. On the other side, there will be small loops. Most of the projects in this book use the loop side as the finished side, with a couple that use the flat stitch. All of the patterns in this book are reversible, but bear in mind if you want to create a design in the future that has the looped stitch as the finished side, you may want to draw your pattern in reverse before tracing it on.

This is particularly important if you want to include words or names in a pattern!

Outline with regular needle: When creating a border or outline of a shape with the regular punch needle, punch in every other hole. This will create a solid line of loops without any gaps **(1)**.

Filling in with regular needle: When filling in a shape or background with the regular needle, punch in every third hole. When you punch your first line, the loops will have gaps in between them. Once your second and third lines are punched next to them, your loops will start to interlock like the teeth on a zip. This can be a little unnerving when you start, but have faith that once your next rows are in, the loops will interlock and close the gaps **(2)**.

When punching, try to ensure that rows sit next to each other covering the fabric so there are no gaps showing through. Stagger your stitches so that they look like bricks on a wall, this will help the loops to interlock **(3)**.

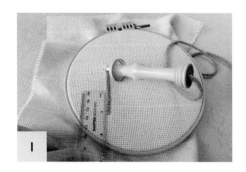

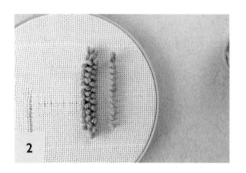

Punching with fine needle: The yarn used for this needle is finer than that of the regular needle, therefore punch in every hole.

How much your yarn fills out on the loopy side will determine how often to leave a gap of a row's width between your rows. You can either punch:

- two rows punched, row's width gap, two rows punched, row's width gap (4).
- one row punched, row's width gap, one row punched, row's width gap (5).

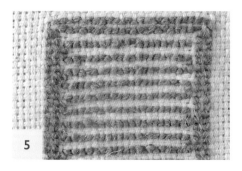

For the two outermost rows punch your rows directly next to each other, when filling in, leave a gap of a row's width.

Small dots: A small dot consists of three stitches. Punch three stitches close together, aiming for a triangle shape. Push the ends of the first and third stitches through (6).

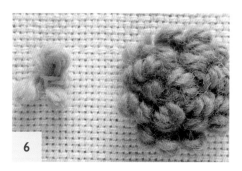

This won't look like a dot until you put in your surrounding stitches. Cut the ends of the first and third stitches flush with your loops.

Finger loops: It is possible to make larger loops than your needle creates by pulling the loops through a little on the other side. These add great texture and are fun to do.

Punch into the fabric as usual, but then use your non-punching hand to go under the fabric and grasp the yarn at the tip of the needle. Pull your needle back through to the top side but keep your fingers in place on the yarn underneath. Continue to punch grasping the yarn on the underneath for each stitch that you wish to be longer (7).

TIDYING UP

When you have finished punching, turn your piece over and take a look at the looped side. Don't worry if this does not look as neat as you envisioned, there are a few things you can do to manipulate the loops and tidy it up.

Snipping ends: All of the tails from the ends of rows will be sticking up above your stitches. Cut these flush to the same height as your other loops **(1)**.

Poke your stitches into place: This isn't a necessary step, but one that I always do at least a little of. If you find once you've cut your ends flush that some of your lines or shapes are a little wobbly, you can do some poking to get more definition. Using the closed end of your embroidery scissors, or your punch needle (unthreaded), push your loops about until they go back where they were intended. I normally only do this for outlines or detailed parts of a design **(2)**.

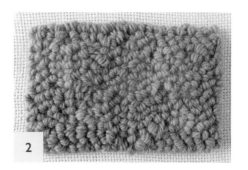

TIPS AND TRICKS

Frogging: If you are not familiar with the term 'frogging', it simply means to pull your work out and do it again. One of the benefits of working with a hard-wearing fabric like monk's cloth is the ability to 'frog' your work. This is great when you are learning, you can test out colours, different types of yarn and different stitches, all safe in the knowledge that if you don't like what you have done you can just pull it out. It is quite a satisfying feeling when the loops pop out of the fabric, so I'd encourage you to have a go **(1)**.

You will find once you have pulled out your loops that the threads have moved apart. It is totally fine to re-punch straight into these widened holes, but if you like, you can use the end of your punch needle to scratch the fabric and spring the threads back into place **(2)**.

PUNCHING INTO AN EMBROIDERY HOOP

As previously mentioned, wooden embroidery hoops are not strong enough to punch straight into, you will end up re-tightening the fabric constantly. However, if you glue your fabric into your hoop, once it is dry you can punch straight into it and then when it is finished it is ready to hang.

Cut a piece of monk's cloth 1¼in (3cm) bigger on each side than the hoop you want to glue it into **(1)**.

Stretch the fabric within the hoop as tight as you can. Use a screwdriver to tighten the screw as tight as possible **(2)**.

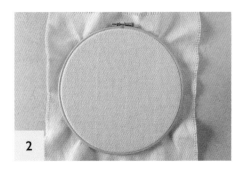

Trim the fabric around the outer hoop so that there is approximately ⅜in (1cm) remaining **(3)**.

Use your fine paintbrush to paint glue on the inside of the inner hoop **(4)**.

Fold the edge of the fabric over and press onto the inner hoop **(5)**.

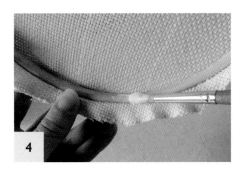

Once the glue is dry, draw your design on and punch!

FINISHING TECHNIQUES

STEAMING

You may find that sometimes when you take your work off the frame, your piece curls in on itself. This is not a bad thing as it means you have punched at the correct tension and your stitches will stay in place. To help with this you can steam / press your work. Before you steam / press your work, check what fibres your yarn is made up of. If you have used a wool- / natural-based yarn, you will be fine to steam it. If you have used an acrylic-based yarn, be careful steaming this and maybe do a tester first – it could melt.

Once you have determined that your yarn is able to be steamed, set up an ironing board and turn your iron on to a setting without steam (you will be creating the steam). With the board and iron set up, fill a large mixing / washing-up bowl with cold water. Take a hand towel and soak it in the water. Then ring it out so that it is not dripping.

Place your piece with the loopy side up, flat on the ironing board. Place the wet hand towel over your piece. Now take the iron and press for approximately 10 seconds on top of the towel.

You should see steam rising from the combination of the cold, wet towel and the hot, dry iron. Repeat this in sections until each part has been pressed (for small pieces like the bookmark or card holder, you will be able to press these with one press of the iron).

Remove the iron and towel and allow your piece to dry.

GLUING

Once you have worked with monk's cloth, you will realise that it frays. When you are punching this can be solved by taping the edges, or securing them with a row of stitching. However, once you have finished punching and want to cut the excess fabric away, you then have the problem of fraying again. If you are making a rug and it is preferable to have a wider hem, you can just double your hem over to hide the frayed edge. For projects where a small hem is preferable, there is a way to seal the edge with glue.

When you have finished punching your piece, taken it off the frame, steamed and left it to dry (if necessary), you can then paint a thin line of glue on to seal the edge. You may want to put something on top of your table to protect it from any glue that may seep through.

Lay your piece on the table, loopy side up, and using a fine paintbrush, paint a ¼in (4mm) wide line of PVA glue approximately ⅜in (1cm) away from the finished edge of punching, all the way around. Leave this to dry (according to the instructions on the glue).

Once dry, take your fabric scissors and cut the fabric along this glued line. You are now ready to hem or finish your project, and this edge will not fray.

Don't forget to rinse and dry your paintbrush afterwards so that it doesn't dry hard!

HEMMING

Learning to hem your punched projects will put you in good stead if you ever want to make a punch needle rug – the technique is the same.

First, glue and cut away the excess fabric according to the measurement in the pattern. Snip the corners off to reduce the bulk of fabric at the corners **(1)**.

With the loopy side face down and the back facing you, fold all of the corners in, followed by the edges, and pin in place. Pull the base fabric as tight as possible so that none will be showing on the right side once you have hemmed **(2)**.

With the base fabric pinned to the wrong side of the piece, thread a needle with a light, neutral thread and stitch the hem in place. When pushing your needle in, make sure to go through the hem and catch a little of the fabric underneath your stitches. This will help you stitch your hem to the base fabric and keep things in place **(3)**.

WHIPPING

An attractive way to finish a piece is by using a whipped edge, often referred to as whip-stitching. The principle is the same whichever project you use it on; a length of yarn and darning needle are used to wrap the edge. This is a particularly useful finishing technique when making a round piece like a trivet, to hide the outer ring of an embroidery hoop or cover the top edge of a basket.

Cut away the excess fabric according to the measurement in the pattern. Roll this fabric in towards the last row of punched stitching and clip in place to hold (1).

Thread a darning needle with a piece of yarn approximately 19¾in (50cm) in length. Push your needle into the fabric from the finished side, as close to the punched stitches as possible. Leave about an inch of yarn exposed and tuck this into the rolled fabric (2).

Bring your needle up and over the rolled edge and insert in close to the previous stitch. Pull the yarn tight as you go. Rethread your needle with yarn as necessary and continue to bind the entire edge with the whip-stitch. Don't be tempted to cut a really long piece of yarn as it is more difficult to work with (3).

SMALL GEOMETRIC CUSHION COVER

Create a cosy nook with this neat cushion cover; the modern abstract pattern makes it perfect for styling a simple chair as a focal point in any room or paired with the Large Geometric Cushion Cover (see page 30) to make a comfy invitation to your sofa or bed.

SKILL LEVEL: MOVING ON

YOU'LL NEED:

- Frame for stretching the fabric – I used a 16in (40.5cm) frame

- Monk's cloth fabric – 19¾in (50cm) square

- Approximately 100g of super bulky Merino wool (CYC group 6)

- #10 Oxford regular punch needle

- Fabric scissors

- Embroidery scissors or snips

- Sewing needle and matching thread

- Tape measure

- Two pieces of backing fabric, 12½in x 7¾in (32cm x 20cm) (I used a wool mix felt)

- 9¾in (25cm) cushion insert

STATIONERY:

- Masking tape

- Permanent marker or pencil

- Plain paper

- PVA (or alternative strong glue) and fine paintbrush

OPTIONAL:

- Lightbox

- Sewing machine

SMALL GEOMETRIC CUSHION COVER

Size: The pattern will make one small cushion cover, which will be 9¾in (25cm) square.

ABOUT THE PROJECT

The looped stitches are visible on the right side of the cushion. A wool mix felt was used to form the envelope closure on the back.

METHOD

To punch the cushion cover

1 Measure and cut a 19¾in (50cm) square piece of monk's cloth.

2 Tape the edges of the fabric with masking tape so the fabric does not fray. Alternatively, you can overlock the edges if you prefer.

3 The cushion cover is square. Draw a 9in (23cm) square on to the centre of the fabric (see the tip on page 14 for how to draw a straight line). You are going to stretch the fabric really tight onto the frame. This will make the fabric 'grow' a little on each side and it will be 9¾in (25cm) when punched.

4 The template for the motif can be found on page 126 and needs to be copied at 200%. Trace the design on to the square (see page 14 for more information on how to effectively trace your designs on to the fabric).

5 Evenly stretch the fabric on to the frame (see page 15 for further instructions) so that the square is central in the frame.

6 The cushion cover is punched using four colours, but you can adapt this to your décor. If you are also making the larger cushion cover, why not punch them both using complementary colours. This Merino wool is super soft so will be comfortable on your back.

7 Start by punching the semi-circle shapes. Thread your regular punch needle in the first colour.

8 Punch in every other hole, along the outline of the circle. This will help to give your outline some definition.

9 Fill in the circle, punching in roughly every third hole (see page 19 for more information on how to fill in with the regular needle).

To sew up the cushion cover

1 The cushion cover will be finished with an envelope back, a very simple backing for a cushion. This cushion cover was sewn using a sewing machine, but you could complete it by hand, it'll just take a little longer.

2 The cushion cover may require a little steaming before you sew it up. Be careful if you have used Merino wool, as you will only want to steam it lightly (see the instructions on steaming on page 23).

3 Once you have finished punching, use your fine paintbrush to paint a line of glue approximately 1¼in (3cm) away from the finished edge. Allow this to dry according to the instructions on the glue.

10 Complete all the semi-circles.

11 Now to fill in the background. Punch the border of the cushion, punching in every other hole. Where the design meets one of the semi-circle shapes, continue punching around it, but using the larger, filling-in stitch. As you have already outlined each semi-circle using the outline stitch (every other hole) you do not need to punch another row in this smaller stitch.

12 With the border punched, fill in the background punching in every third hole.

13 When you have finished punching, turn over the frame and snip off all of the ends. If you would like neat lines, poke any stitches that need a little refinement into place.

4 Once dry, cut your cushion cover along this glued edge. This will stop the fabric from fraying. Cut two rectangles out of your backing fabric, 12½in x 7¾in (32cm x 20cm). I used wool mix felt as it does not fray and so does not require hemming before use. It's a nice, easy fabric to sew with as a beginner.

5 The two pieces of felt will overlap and this will form your envelope closure.

6 Next we will begin to sew the cushion up. You can either use a sewing machine or sew by hand. For either, make sure to use a small, straight stitch.

7 You will first sew a small hem on to each piece of backing fabric.

8 Along one long edge of each piece of backing fabric, fold over ⅜in (1cm), pin and sew a straight line of stitching.

9 Place the punched piece flat on a table with the loopy (right) side facing up. Place the two pieces of backing felt, right side down, on to the punched piece. The long edges without the hems should line up with the outer edge of your monk's cloth. The long edges that you hemmed should overlap in the middle by 2½in (7cm). This overlap forms the envelope opening.

10 Pin the backing fabric and the punched piece together all the way around the edge.

11 If using a sewing machine to stitch together, use a zipper foot so that you can sew as close as possible all the way around the cushion's edge. If stitching by hand, you'll be able to get pretty close.

12 Remove the pins, turn your cushion right side out and put in the cushion insert.

LARGE GEOMETRIC CUSHION COVER

Inject some cool, contemporary style into your living room with this bold abstract patterned cushion cover – choose colours to co-ordinate with your décor or contrast to create a statement piece. Why not try teaming it with the Small Geometric Cushion Cover (see page 26) if you really want to make a display of your skills.

SKILL LEVEL: MOVING ON

YOU'LL NEED:

- Frame for stretching the fabric – I used a 21in (53.5cm) frame

- Monk's cloth fabric – 24¾in (63cm) square

- Approximately 280g of super bulky Merino wool (CYC group 6)

- #10 Oxford regular punch needle

- Fabric scissors

- Embroidery scissors or snips

- Sewing needle and matching thread

- Tape measure

- Two pieces of backing fabric, 18in (46cm) x 12½in (32cm) (I used a wool mix felt)

- 15¾in (40cm) cushion insert

STATIONERY:

- Masking tape

- Permanent marker or pencil

- Plain paper

- PVA (or alternative strong glue) and fine paintbrush

OPTIONAL:

- Lightbox

- Sewing machine

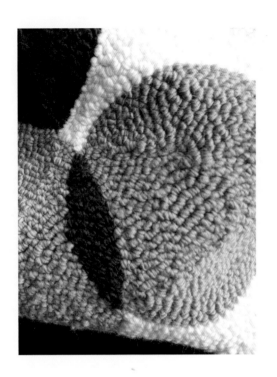

LARGE GEOMETRIC CUSHION COVER

Size: The pattern will make one large cushion cover, which will be 15¾in (40cm) square.

ABOUT THE PROJECT

The looped stitches are visible on the right side of the cushion. A wool mix felt was used to form the envelope closure on the back.

METHOD

To punch the cushion cover

1 Measure and cut a 24¾in (63cm) square piece of monk's cloth.

2 Tape the edges of the fabric with masking tape so the fabric does not fray. Alternatively, you can overlock the edges if you prefer.

3 The cushion cover is square. Draw a 15in (38cm) square on to the centre of the fabric (see the tip on page 14 for how to draw a straight line). You are going to stretch the fabric really tightly on to the frame. This will make the fabric 'grow' a little on each side and it will be 15¾in (40cm) when punched.

4 The template for the motif can be found on page 127 and needs to be copied at 220%. Trace the design on to the square (see page 14 for more information on how to effectively trace your designs on to the fabric).

5 Evenly stretch the fabric on to the frame (see page 15 for further instructions), so that the square is central in the frame.

6 The cushion cover is punched using five colours, but you can adapt it to your décor. If you are also making the small cushion cover, why not punch them using complementary colours? This Merino wool is super soft, so will be comfortable on your back.

7 Start by punching the circular shapes. Thread your regular punch needle in the first colour.

8 Punch in every other hole along the outline of the shape. This will help to give your outline some definition.

9 Fill in the shape, punching in roughly every third hole (see page 19 for more information on how to fill in with the regular needle).

To sew up the cushion cover

1 The cushion cover will be finished with an envelope back, a very simple backing for a cushion. This cushion cover was sewn using a sewing machine, but you could complete it by hand, it'll just take a little longer.

2 The cushion cover may require a little steaming before you sew it up. Be careful if you have used Merino wool, as you will only want to steam it lightly (see the instructions on steaming on page 23).

3 Once you have finished punching, use your fine paintbrush to paint a line of glue approximately 1¼in (3cm) away from the finished edge. Allow this to dry (according to the instructions on the glue).

10 Complete all the shapes.

11 Now to fill in the background. Punch the border of the cushion, punching in every other hole. Where the design meets one of the shapes, continue punching around it, but using the larger filling-in stitch. As you have already outlined each shape using the outline stitch (every other hole) you do not need to punch another row in this smaller stitch.

12 With the border punched, fill in the background punching in every third hole.

13 When you have finished punching, turn over the frame and snip off all the ends. If you would like neat lines, poke any stitches that need a little refinement into place.

4 Once dry, cut your cushion cover along this glued edge. It will stop the fabric from fraying.

5 Cut two rectangles out of your backing fabric, 18in (46cm) × 12½in (32cm). I used wool mix felt as it does not fray and so does not require hemming before use. It's a nice, easy fabric to sew with as a beginner.

6 The two pieces of felt will overlap and this will form your envelope closure.

7 Next, we will begin to sew the cushion up. You can either use a sewing machine or can sew by hand. For either, make sure to use a small, straight stitch.

8 You will first sew a small hem on to each piece of backing fabric.

9 Along one long edge of each piece of backing fabric, fold over ⅜in (1cm), pin and sew a straight line of stitching.

10 Place the punched piece flat on a table with the loopy (right) side facing up.

11 Place the two pieces of backing felt, right side down, on to the punched piece. The long edges without the hems should line up with the outer edge of your monk's cloth. The long edges that you hemmed should overlap in the middle by 6½in (16cm). This overlap forms the envelope opening.

12 Pin the backing fabric and the punched piece together all the way around the edge.

13 If using a sewing machine to stitch together, use a zipper foot so that you can sew as close as possible all the way around the cushion's edge. If stitching by hand, you'll be able to get pretty close.

14 Remove the pins and turn your cushion right side out and put in the cushion insert.

HANDBAG

Add a touch of vintage style to your look with this cute retro handbag. It's a perfect size to hold all your essential items, so you'll have everything you need. The simple, easy-to-hold wooden handles are a practical and attractive feature.

SKILL LEVEL: MOVING ON

YOU'LL NEED:

- Frame for stretching the fabric – I used a 12in (30.5cm) no-slip hoop

- Monk's cloth fabric – 2 x 15in (38cm) square

- Approximately 170g of bulky-weight yarn (CYC group 5)

- #10 Oxford regular punch needle

- Fabric scissors

- Embroidery scissors or snips

- Sewing needle and matching thread

- Darning needle

- Tape measure

- Pair of wooden bag handles size approximately 6¼in (16cm) at the widest point, with an internal hole height approximately 2¼in (5.5cm)

STATIONERY:

- Masking tape

- Permanent marker or pencil

- Plain paper

- PVA (or alternative strong glue) and fine paintbrush

OPTIONAL:

- Lightbox

HANDBAG

Size: The bag will be 7in (18cm) at the widest point and 7¾in (20cm) at the tallest point.

ABOUT THE PROJECT

The looped stitches are visible on the right sides of the bag. The punched part is finished with a small hem and then wooden handles are attached at the opening.

METHOD

To punch the handbag

1 Measure and cut two 15in (38cm) square pieces of monk's cloth.

2 Tape the edges of the fabric with masking tape so the fabric does not fray. Alternatively, you can overlock the edges if you prefer.

3 The template for the motif can be found on pages 136 and 137. Trace the front design on to one piece of fabric and the back design on to the other. Decide which side you will punch first. (See page 14 for more information on how to effectively trace your designs on to the fabric.)

4 Evenly stretch the fabric on to the hoop (see page 15 for further instructions) so the design is central in the hoop.

5 All of the organic shapes are similar in that they touch other shapes and form part of the border, so you can punch them in any order you choose.

6 Thread your needle with the first colour and outline the shape, punching in every other hole.

7 Continue with this colour and fill in the shape, following the outline inwards, punching in every third hole.

8 Continue to punch in this manner for the rest of the shapes.

9 When you have punched one side of the bag, remove it from the hoop and repeat for the other side.

10 Push all of the ends through to the right side and snip.

11 Poke any loops that need further refinement into place.

To finish the handbag

The handbag will be finished with a small hem on the reverse side. Wooden handles will be attached to the top of the opening.

1 Using a fine paintbrush and PVA glue, paint a line of glue ½in (1.5cm) away from the finished piece to create a border and allow to dry. Paint this line at least ¼in (0.5cm) thick along the curved edge. You will need to snip into this edge to ensure it doesn't pucker when you hem it.

2 Once dry, cut along the outside of the glued edge to stop the fabric from fraying.

3 Along the curved edge snip into the outline at roughly ⅜in (1cm) intervals.

4 Pin and stitch the hem in place. Complete this for both sides of the bag.

5 Place the wrong sides (flat stitches) of the bag together and clip to hold in place. You will need to clip along the two long sides and the curved edge. There is no need to clip the shorter edges together as this will become the opening of the bag.

6 Using a needle and thread in a similar colour to your yarn, use small whip-stitches to stitch the two long edges and the curved edge together.

7 Decide which colour yarn you would like to use to attach the wooden handles and cut two pieces that are 59in (150cm) in length.

8 Thread one piece of the yarn on to a darning needle. On the inside edge of the opening of the bag, insert the needle into the hem and knot.

9 Using a whip-stitch, attach the handle to the top of the bag with the yarn – the yarn should be stitched over at least 20 times. Make your stitches sit slightly apart so you can still see the handle. Once at the other end of the opening, knot the yarn on the inside edge of the bag.

10 Repeat for the other handle.

TOOL TUB

Keep threads and small work tools safely in one place in this pretty little pot, ensuring you always have everything you need to hand and its neat size means it's not going to take up too much room wherever you choose to work. Why not make a matching duo with the Large Storage Tub (see page 42).

SKILL LEVEL: MOVING ON

YOU'LL NEED:

- Frame for stretching the fabric – I used a 16in (40.5cm) canvas stretcher bar frame

- Monk's cloth fabric – 17¾in (45cm) square

- Approximately 120g of bulky-weight yarn (CYC group 5)

- Oxford #10 regular punch needle

- Fabric scissors

- Embroidery scissors

- Darning needle

- Sewing needle and matching thread

- Tape measure

- 7¾in (20cm) square piece of felt

STATIONERY:

- Masking tape

- Permanent marker or pencil

- Plain paper

- PVA (or alternative strong glue) and paintbrush

OPTIONAL:

- Lightbox

- Sewing machine

TOOL TUB

Size: 4¼in (11cm) tall and 12¼in (31cm) in diameter.

ABOUT THE PROJECT

The flat stitches form the finished side of the tool pot and the bottom is made from felt fabric.

METHOD

To punch the tool tub

1 Measure and cut a 17¾in (45cm) square piece of monk's cloth.

2 Tape the edges of the fabric with masking tape so the fabric does not fray. Alternatively, you can overlock the edges if you prefer.

3 Leaving at least a 4in (10cm) border of monk's cloth for stretching on to the frame, draw out a rectangle 11¾in × 4in (30 × 10cm) on the monk's cloth (see the tip on page 14 to get a perfectly straight line!)

4 The template for the motif can be found on page 128. Trace the motif on to the rectangle, leaving a gap of approximately 1¼in (3cm) in between each motif (see page 14 for more information on how to effectively trace your designs on to the fabric).

5 Evenly stretch the fabric on to the frame (see page 15 for further instructions).

6 Starting with the mustard shapes, punch the outline, punching in every other hole (see page 16 for further instructions on punching).

7 Following the outline and spiralling into the centre continue punching, filling in the rest of the shape, punching in every third hole.

8 Once at the centre of the shape, pull the punch needle up to expose ⅜in (1cm) of yarn.

9 Cut the yarn off and using the closed, pointed end of the embroidery scissors, push the small piece of yarn through to the loopy side.

10 Continue punching all of the mustard shapes.

To finish the tool tub

1 The tool pot will have a small piece of fabric as a base with the top edge whipped.

2 Using a fine paintbrush and PVA glue, paint a line of glue 1¼in (3.5cm) away from the finished piece to create a border. Allow to dry.

3 Once dry, cut along the glued line, trimming the excess fabric away. This will ensure that your fabric doesn't fray.

4 Place the right sides together (the sides with the flat stitches) and pin in place.

5 Sew a line of straight stitches along the short edges, attaching them together. If you are using a sewing machine, a zipper foot will help you to get as close as you can to the punched stitches.

6 Cut a 5½in (14cm) diameter circle out of fabric. I used a wool mix felt.

7 Round the edge of the circle, make snips roughly ⅜in (1cm) long, approximately ⅜in (1cm) apart. These will help you to tack the circle in place on to the bottom of the pot, without puckering the fabric.

8 Pin the felt circle to the bottom of the pot and hand stitch around to secure in place.

9 Turn out the pot so that the right side is facing outwards.

10 If you find any exposed monk's cloth along the short edge that you sewed together, take a darning needle, thread with the background colour yarn and whip-stitch from one edge to the other to cover the monk's cloth.

11 Fold the border of fabric at the top over on itself twice and use pegs to hold in place. Using the same yarn as the background colour, go around the top of the pot and whip-stitch over the edge of monk's cloth, covering it all (see page 25 for instructions on how to whip the edge).

11 Once all punched, change your yarn to the white and punch the white circles first with the outline and then fill in.

12 When all of the shapes are punched, start punching the background.

13 Begin with the outline of the rectangle, then outline each of the shapes with the speckled brown. Now you are ready to fill in the remaining background.

14 If you find yourself in a dead end, snip your yarn off and re-start punching in the next area, don't jump over stitches.

(If you are using the additional fabric on the frame to make another project, punch this first before removing from the frame.)

Tips

You'll have enough space on a 15¾in (40cm) square frame to punch two of these tubs if you draw your rectangles with a gap of 3in (8cm) in the middle for hemming. If you don't want two, why not use the extra fabric to punch one of the smaller projects like the passport holder or pin cushion.

Use the guidelines on the fabric when stretching to ensure that your pattern is straight.

The flat stitches will form the finished side of this pot, so try to get your stitches close together and cover all the fabric.

LARGE STORAGE TUB

This super-sized tub is just the job for keeping your workspace neat and tidy and in giving all your odds and ends a stylish place to live. The motif pairs perfectly with the Tool Tub (see page 38). Use them together for all your storage needs around the home.

SKILL LEVEL: MOVING ON

YOU'LL NEED:

- Frame for stretching the fabric – I used a 28in (71cm) canvas stretcher bar frame

- Monk's cloth fabric – 29½in (75cm) square (this will make two tubs)

- Approximately 300g of bulky-weight yarn (CYC group 5) (or 600g if you want to make two)

- #10 Oxford regular punch needle

- Fabric scissors

- Embroidery scissors or snips

- Sewing needle and matching thread

- Tape measure

- 11¾in (30cm) square piece of felt

STATIONERY:

- Masking tape

- Permanent marker or pencil

- Plain paper

- PVA (or alternative strong glue) and fine paintbrush

OPTIONAL:

- Lightbox

LARGE STORAGE TUB

Size: The fabric will make two large storage tubs, which will be 6in (15cm) tall and approximately 7¾in (20cm) in diameter. If you don't want to make two tubs, consider drawing out some of the smaller projects on to the excess fabric.

ABOUT THE PROJECT

The looped stitches are visible on the outside of the storage tub and form the right side. There is a small hem underneath to finish off the fabric, with the bottom of the tub made from a wool mix fabric.

METHOD

To punch the storage tub

1 Measure and cut a 29½in (75cm) square piece of monk's cloth.

2 Tape the edges of the fabric with masking tape so the fabric does not fray. Alternatively, you can overlock the edges if you prefer.

3 The storage tub is made using a rectangle. Draw a 23½in x 6in (60 x 15cm) rectangle on to the centre of the fabric (if drawing two, leave a gap of 4in (10cm) in between them).

4 The template for the motif can be found on page 128. Trace the motif on to the rectangle leaving a gap of approximately 1¼in (3cm) in between each motif. For the large tub the motif alternates and is flipped upside down to add some interest. (See page 14 for more information on how to effectively trace your designs on to the fabric).

5 Evenly stretch the fabric on to the frame (see page 15 for further instructions) so that the designs are central in the frame.

6 You will notice there is a white border along the circumference of the tub – we will punch this part first.

7 Thread your needle with the border colour and punch along each long side of the rectangle, punching in every other hole. Punch two rows close together along the top and bottom edges.

8 For the circles and motifs, once your needle is threaded with a particular colour, punch all of these sections in one go.

To finish the large storage tub

1 The storage tub will have a piece of fabric as a base. I used a wool mix felt as the texture works well with the yarn and it's an easy fabric to work with.

2 Using a fine paintbrush and PVA glue, paint a line of glue 1¼in (3.5cm) away from the finished piece to create a border. Allow to dry.

3 Once dry, cut along the glued line, trimming the excess fabric away. This will ensure that your fabric doesn't fray.

4 Before sewing the tub up you will need to hem one of the long edges.

5 Pin and hem one of the long edges.

9 Punch in every other hole for the outline of the shapes and then fill in, punching in roughly every third hole (see page 19 for more information on how to fill in with the regular needle).

10 With all of the inner objects punched, now start on the background. For the short edges that you did not outline in white, use the background colour and punch in every other hole for the first two rows.

11 Fill in the rest of the background, punching in every third hole.

6 Place the right sides together (the loopy sides) and pin in place.

7 Sew a line of straight stitches along the short edges, attaching them together. If you are using a sewing machine a zipper foot will help you to get as close as you can to the punched stitches.

8 Cut out an 11¾in (30cm) diameter circle of fabric. I used a wool mix felt.

9 Around the edge of the circle make snips roughly ⅜in (1cm) long, approximately ⅜in (1cm) apart. These will help you to tack the circle in place on to the bottom of the tub without puckering the fabric.

10 Pin the felt circle to the bottom of the tub and hand stitch around to secure in place.

11 Turn the tub out so that the right side is facing outwards.

12 If you find any exposed monk's cloth along the short edge that you sewed together, take a darning needle, thread with the background colour yarn and whip-stitch from one edge to the other to cover the monk's cloth (see page 25 for instructions on how to whip the edge).

GEOMETRIC WALL ART

Make this circular picture to highlight any wall in your home – a simple ruler or straight edge is all you need to create the angular shapes and parallel lines to fill with colour. Worked on an embroidery hoop that remains an integral part of the design, it creates an interesting detail and feature.

SKILL LEVEL: MOVING ON

YOU'LL NEED:

- 10in (25.5cm) embroidery hoop

- Monk's cloth fabric – 11¾in (30cm) square

- Approximately 110g of bulky-weight yarn (CYC group 5)

- #10 Oxford regular punch needle

- Fabric scissors

- Embroidery scissors or snips

- Darning needle

- Tape measure

STATIONERY:

- Ruler

- Permanent marker or pencil

- PVA (or alternative strong glue) and fine paintbrush

GEOMETRIC WALL ART

Size: The wall hanging will be made using a 10in (25.5cm) embroidery hoop and this will be the finished size.

ABOUT THE PROJECT

The flat stitches will be visible on the finished side of the hoop, with the outer hoop covered in yarn.

METHOD

To punch the wall hanging

Unlike some of the other projects where you will work in a frame or hoop, remove your project and finish it in another way, this wall hanging will be made in the embroidery hoop and then remain in there for finishing.

1 Measure and cut an 11¾in (30cm) square piece of monk's cloth.

2 You do not need to do anything to secure the edges of the fabric as you will be gluing it to the hoop.

3 Follow the instructions on page 22 (punching into an embroidery hoop) to see how to stretch and glue your fabric into the hoop.

4 You will be punching on to the front of the hoop so that the flat stitches are visible. They help to accentuate the angular nature of the design.

5 The design for this hoop was created using a ruler, but you can use anything with a straight edge.

6 Once the glue is dry, with the hoop facing upwards, place your ruler at an angle and draw multiple lines on to the fabric. This will form your design. You can draw as many or as few lines as you like. Bear in mind the more lines you draw, the more sections you will need to complete. Place your lines at angles to each other, make different widths of shapes, some with thicker ends and others that come together in a point. Plan your design so that no two colours are next to each other. Have fun with creating your unique angular design.

To finish the wall art

The outer edge of the embroidery hoop is covered using yarn and a whip-stitch.

The lines of the design are carried on from the centre over the edge of the hoop. Follow the instructions on page 25 (whipping) to cover the edge of the embroidery hoop with yarn.

7 Thread your needle with your yarn and punch the different sections. Start with the outline first and then fill in. You will want to keep your stitches as close as possible and ensure that all of the fabric is covered (see page 19 for more information on different stitches).

8 When you have finished punching, turn over the hoop and snip off all the ends flush with the loops.

9 As the flat stitches are visible on the front you will not need to do any tidying up of stitches.

PIN CUSHION

A pin cushion is a useful piece of kit for anyone who sews, and this super-stylish modern design would make an ideal gift. With its easy skill level and neat size it makes the perfect project if you're new to this craft, and it won't take you forever to make.

SKILL LEVEL: EASY

YOU'LL NEED:

- Frame for stretching the fabric – I used a 7in (18cm) no-slip hoop

- Monk's cloth fabric – 9½in (24cm) square

- Approximately 30g of bulky-weight yarn (CYC group 5)

- #10 Oxford regular punch needle

- Fabric scissors

- Embroidery scissors or snips

- Sewing needle and matching thread

- Tape measure

- One small piece of backing fabric, 4½ x 6in (11.5 x 15cm) (I used a wool mix felt)

- Small amount of recycled polyester toy filling

STATIONERY:

- Masking tape

- Permanent marker or pencil

- Plain paper

- PVA (or alternative strong glue) and fine paintbrush

OPTIONAL:

- Lightbox

PIN CUSHION

Size: The pattern will make one small pin cushion, which will be 4in × 2¾in (10 × 7cm).

ABOUT THE PROJECT

The looped stitches are visible on the right side of the pin cushion. A wool mix felt was used for the backing.

METHOD

To punch the pin cushion

1 Measure and cut a 9½in (24cm) square piece of monk's cloth (see Tips, page 53).

2 Tape the edges of the fabric with masking tape so the fabric does not fray. Alternatively, you can overlock the edges if you prefer.

3 Draw a 4in × 2¾in (10 × 7cm) rectangle on to the centre of the fabric (see the tip on page 14 for how to draw a straight line).

4 The template for the motif can be found on page 129. Trace the design on to the rectangle (see page 14 for more information on how to effectively trace your designs on to the fabric).

5 Evenly stretch the fabric on to the hoop (see page 15 for further instructions) so that the design is central in the hoop.

6 All of the shapes in this design are quite equal, they all touch other shapes and they all contribute to the border.

7 Decide which shape you will punch first and thread your needle with that colour yarn.

8 Punch in every other hole along the outline of the shape. This will help to give your outline some definition (see page 19 for more information on outlining with regular needle).

9 Once outlined, fill in the shape, punching in every third hole (see page 19 for more information on how to fill in with the regular needle).

To finish the pin cushion

1 The pin cushion needs a small amount of backing fabric and filling to be completed. It is easiest to complete the sewing by hand.

2 Once you have finished punching, use your fine paintbrush to paint a line of glue approximately ⅜in (1cm) away from the finished edge. Allow this to dry according to the instructions on the glue.

3 Once dry, cut your pin cushion along this glued edge, to stop the fabric from fraying.

10 Punch the rest of the shapes in the same manner.

11 When you have finished punching, turn over the hoop and snip off all of the ends. If you would like neat lines, poke any stitches that need a little refinement into place.

4 Cut one 6in x 4½in (15 x 11.5cm) rectangle out of your backing fabric. I used wool mix felt as it does not fray and so does not require hemming before use. It's a nice, easy fabric to sew with as a beginner. The backing fabric will be cut slightly larger than the punched piece as this will make it easier to sew up.

5 Place the backing fabric on the table.

6 Place the punched piece on to the fabric with the loopy side (right side) facing downwards.

7 Pin the two pieces together.

8 Thread your needle with a thread of a similar colour to your backing material.

9 Hand-sew three of the sides together, the two long sides and one short end.

10 With three of the sides sewn together, turn the pin cushion so the right side is facing outwards.

11 Stuff the pin cushion through the gap using a recycled polyester toy filling (see Tips, below).

12 Once it is fully stuffed, sew the remaining gap with a row of small whip-stitches (see page 24).

Tips

This is a very small project and will most likely fit on to a piece of left-over monk's cloth from a larger project.

If you don't have any toy filling, why not save up all your yarn ends and stuff with those instead.

SMALL PLANT POT COVER

This gorgeous little plant pot cover will sit neatly over an existing small planter to brighten up a dull shelf or create an eye-catching feature on an uninspiring hallway windowsill. It would look fabulous as a set of three.

SKILL LEVEL: EASY

YOU'LL NEED:

- Frame for stretching the fabric – I used a 12in (30.5cm) no-slip hoop

- Monk's cloth fabric – 14¼in (37cm) square

- Approximately 100g of medium-weight yarn (CYC group 4)

- #14 Oxford fine punch needle

- Fabric scissors

- Embroidery scissors or snips

- Sewing needle and matching thread

- Tape measure

STATIONERY:

- Masking tape

- Permanent marker or pencil

- Plain paper

- PVA (or alternative strong glue) and fine paintbrush

OPTIONAL:

- Lightbox

SMALL PLANT POT COVER

Size: The pattern will make a plant pot cover that will be 8¾in (22.5cm) in length, 3in (7.5cm) in height with approximately 2¾in (7cm) wide diameter when stitched.

ABOUT THE PROJECT

The looped stitches are visible on the outside of the plant pot cover and form the right side. The plant pot cover is adjustable, with the short ends drawn together using a colourful piece of yarn.

METHOD

To punch the plant pot cover

1 Measure and cut a 14¼in (37cm) square piece of monk's cloth. (There will be space on the fabric for another small project, so why not punch the pin cushion or card holder whilst you're at it!)

2 Tape the edges of the fabric with masking tape so the fabric does not fray. Alternatively, you can overlock the edges if you prefer.

3 The plant pot cover is a rectangle. Draw a rectangle 8¾in × 3in (22.5cm × 7.5cm) on to the fabric, roughly in the centre. If you are drawing on another project, ensure you leave at least a 2in (5cm) gap for the hems.

4 The template for the motif can be found on page 129. Trace the simple shell-like design on to the fabric (see page 14 for more information on how to effectively trace your designs on to the fabric).

5 Evenly stretch the fabric on to the hoop (see page 15 for further instructions).

6 The plant pot cover is punched using five colours here, but you could always use fewer or more (see Tip, page 57).

7 You will outline and fill each section in turn.

8 Thread your needle with the first colour. Punching in every hole, outline the first shape.

9 Punch another line directly inside this first row of punching so that you now have two rows of punching beside each other.

10 Leave a gap of roughly one row.

11 Continue to punch in this fashion, two rows beside each other, leaving a gap of one row.

To finish the small plant pot cover

1 The plant pot cover will be finished using a small hem on the inside. Then the short ends will be drawn together with a small piece of yarn to make the cover adjustable.

2 As the plant pot cover has been punched using the fine needle and medium-weight yarn, it most likely will not need any steaming.

3 Once you have finished punching, use your fine paintbrush to paint a line of glue approximately ⅜in (1cm) away from the finished edge. Allow this to dry according to the instructions on the glue.

12 Once in the centre of the shape, snip your yarn and push the end through to the right (loopy) side.

13 Repeat for the other shapes until they are all punched.

4 Once dry, cut your plant pot cover along this glued edge, it will stop the fabric from fraying.

5 Hem the plant pot cover with a ⅜in (1cm) hem (following the hemming instructions on page 23).

6 Thread a darning needle with a piece of yarn approximately 11¾in (30cm) long.

7 Hold the cover with the wrong sides together (the loops facing outwards) and the short ends flush.

8 Using your darning needle, weave the yarn from one end of the cover into the other, criss-crossing over a few times and coming back down the other side to form laces as for a corset.

9 Place your plant pot cover over your plant pot and with the two ends of yarn at the bottom, you can now draw the short ends of the cover together and tie with a bow.

> *Tip*
>
> This is a great project for using up small amounts of yarn. Why not make it totally random and use a completely different colour for each section!

LARGE PLANT POT COVER

Make this cool cover for a large planter; its textured effect against leafy foliage will create an interesting statement piece for any room or hallway. Choose tonal shades to blend in with your home décor or pick out contrasting shades to create a pop!

SKILL LEVEL: EASY

YOU'LL NEED:

- Frame for stretching the fabric – I used a 16in (40.5cm) canvas stretcher bar frame

- Monk's cloth fabric – 19¾in (50cm) square (this will make two planters)

- Approximately 120g of bulky-weight yarn (CYC group 5) (or 240g if you want to make two)

- #10 Oxford regular punch needle

- Fabric scissors

- Embroidery scissors or snips

- Sewing needle and matching thread

- Tape measure

STATIONERY:

- Masking tape

- Permanent marker or pencil

- Plain paper

- PVA (or alternative strong glue) and fine paintbrush

OPTIONAL:

- Lightbox

LARGE PLANT POT COVER

Size: The pattern will make two plant pot covers that will be 11¾in (30cm) in length, 4in (10cm) in height, with approximately 4in (10cm) wide diameter when stitched.

ABOUT THE PROJECT

The looped stitches are visible on the outside of the plant pot cover and form the right side. There is a small hem underneath to finish off the fabric, with the ends stitched together to form a tube.

METHOD

To punch the large plant pot cover

1 Measure and cut a 19¾in (50cm) square piece of monk's cloth.

2 Tape the edges of the fabric with masking tape so the fabric does not fray. Alternatively, you can overlock the edges if you prefer.

3 The plant pot cover is a rectangle. Draw two 11¾in x 4in (30cm x 10cm) rectangles (if you want to make two) on to the centre of the fabric. Leave a gap of 2in (5cm) in between the two rectangles for the hem.

4 The template for the motif can be found on page 129 and needs to be copied at 200%. Trace the motif on to the rectangle, leaving a gap of approximately 1¼in (3cm) in between each motif (see page 14 for more information on how to effectively trace your designs on to the fabric).

5 Evenly stretch the fabric on to the frame (see page 15 for further instructions) so that the designs are central in the frame.

6 The plant pot cover is punched using three colours here, but you could always incorporate more.

7 Start with punching the circles. Thread your regular punch needle in the first colour.

8 Punch in every other hole along the outline of the circle. This will help to give your outline some definition.

9 Fill in the circle, punching in roughly every third hole (see page 19 for more information on how to fill in with the regular needle).

To finish the large plant pot cover

1 The plant pot cover will be finished using a small hem on the inside, with the short ends stitched together to form a tube.

2 The plant pot cover may require a little steaming before you sew the hems (see the instructions on steaming on page 23).

3 Once you have finished punching, use your fine paintbrush to paint a line of glue approximately ⅜in (1cm) away from the finished edge. Allow this to dry according to the instructions on the glue.

4 Once dry, cut your plant pot cover along this glued edge. It will stop the fabric from fraying.

5 Hem the plant pot cover with a ⅜in (1cm) hem (following the hemming instructions on page 23).

6 Now that the cover is hemmed you need to stitch the short ends together to form the tube. It is easier to do this with the wrong sides together.

7 With the short ends together and the loops (right side) facing outwards, use a neutral thread and needle to stitch the ends together.

10 Complete all the circles in this colour whilst your needle is still threaded.

11 Repeat for the other circles.

12 Now punch the outline of each of the larger motifs, punching in every other hole.

13 Fill in the large motifs, punching in every third hole.

14 With all of the inner objects punched, now start on the background. Punch the outline of the rectangle, punching in every other hole.

15 Fill in the background, punching in every third hole.

DOORSTOP

A handy doorstop that's sure to catch the eye and envy of all who come to visit your home. For added functionality, use a neutral palette of colours so that it will co-ordinate with the décor of any room in your home.

SKILL LEVEL: EASY

YOU'LL NEED:

- Frame for stretching the fabric — I used a 12in (30.5cm) no-slip hoop

- Monk's cloth fabric — 15¾in (40cm) square

- Approximately 90g of bulky-weight yarn (CYC group 5)

- #10 Oxford regular punch needle

- Fabric scissors

- Embroidery scissors or snips

- Sewing needle and matching thread

- Tape measure

- One small piece of backing fabric, 7½in x 9½in (19 x 24 cm) (I used a wool mix felt)

- Dried rice or alternative filling

STATIONERY:

- Masking tape

- Permanent marker or pencil

- Plain paper

- PVA (or alternative strong glue) and fine paintbrush

OPTIONAL:

- Lightbox

DOORSTOP

Size: The pattern will make one doorstop that will be 7¾in x 6in (20 x 15cm).

ABOUT THE PROJECT

The looped stitches are visible on the right side of the doorstop. A wool mix felt was used for the backing and the filling was dried rice.

METHOD

To punch the doorstop

1 Measure and cut a 15¾in (40cm) square piece of monk's cloth.

2 Tape the edges of the fabric with masking tape so the fabric does not fray. Alternatively, you can overlock the edges if you prefer.

3 Draw a 7¾in x 6in (20 x 15cm) rectangle on to the centre of the fabric (see the tip on page 14 for how to draw a straight line).

4 The template for the motif can be found on page 128 and needs to be copied at 111%. Trace the design on to the rectangle (see page 14 for more information on how to effectively trace your designs on to the fabric).

5 Evenly stretch the fabric on to the hoop (see page 15 for further instructions) so that the design is central in the hoop.

6 The three semi-circles are relatively equal in size. It is best to start with the full semi-circle at the bottom and work your way upwards with the background to be punched last.

7 Thread your needle with the colour for the bottom semi-circle.

8 Punch in every other hole along the outline of the shape. This will help to give your outline some definition. (See page 19 for more information on outlining with the regular needle).

9 Once outlined, fill in the shape, punching in every third hole (see page 19 for more information on how to fill in with the regular needle).

10 Punch the other two semi-circles in the same manner.

To finish the doorstop

1 The doorstop needs a backing and filling to be completed. It is easiest to complete the sewing by hand.

2 Once you have finished punching, use your fine paintbrush to paint a line of glue approximately ⅜in (1cm) away from the finished edge. Allow this to dry according to the instructions on the glue.

3 Once dry, cut your doorstop along this glued edge. It will stop the fabric from fraying.

4 Cut one 9½in x 7½in (24 x 19cm) rectangle out of your backing fabric. I used wool mix felt as it does not fray and so does not require hemming before use.

11 Now to fill in the background. Punch the border of the doorstop, punching in every other hole. Where it meets one of the semi-circle shapes, continue punching around it, but using the larger, filling-in stitch. As you have already outlined each semi-circle using the outline stitch (every other hole) you do not need to punch another row in this smaller stitch.

12 With the border punched, fill in the background, punching in every third hole.

13 When you have finished punching, turn over the hoop and snip off all of the ends. If you would like neat lines, poke any stitches into place that need a little refinement.

It's a nice, easy fabric to sew with as a beginner. The backing fabric will be cut slightly larger than the punched piece as this will make it easier to sew up.

5 Place the backing fabric on the table.

6 Place the punched piece on to the fabric with the loopy side (right side) facing downwards.

7 Pin the two pieces together.

8 Thread your needle with a thread in a similar colour to your backing material.

9 Hand-sew three of the sides together, the two long sides and the bottom edge (with the full semi-circle).

10 With three of the sides sewn together, turn the doorstop so the right side is facing outwards.

11 Fill the doorstop with dried rice (or other heavy filling) through the gap at the top.

12 Once it is filled, sew the remaining edge at the top with a row of small whip-stitches (see page 25).

PENDANT WALL HANGING

Create your own piece of art with this pendant wall hanging. It requires a little more skill than some of the easier pieces, but it really is worth the effort as the bold colours and simple design are guaranteed to add interest to any plain wall.

SKILL LEVEL: MOVING ON

YOU'LL NEED:

- Frame for stretching the fabric – I used a 12in (30.5cm) no-slip hoop

- Monk's cloth fabric – 15in (38cm) square

- Approximately 100g of bulky-weight yarn (CYC group 5)

- #10 Oxford regular punch needle

- Fabric scissors

- Embroidery scissors or snips

- Sewing needle and matching thread

- Darning needle

- Tape measure

- Wooden dowel – 9½in (24cm) length x ½in (2mm) thick

STATIONERY:

- Masking tape

- Permanent marker or pencil

- Plain paper

- PVA (or alternative strong glue) and fine paintbrush

OPTIONAL:

- Lightbox

PENDANT WALL HANGING

Size: The pendant will be 8¾in (22cm) in length and 7in (18cm) wide at the widest point.

ABOUT THE PROJECT

The looped stitches are visible on the right side of the pendant. It is hemmed on the back and hung via a wooden dowel at the top.

METHOD

To punch the pendant hanging

1 Measure and cut a 15in (38cm) square piece of monk's cloth.

2 Tape the edges of the fabric with masking tape so the fabric does not fray. Alternatively, you can overlock the edges if you prefer.

3 The template for the motif can be found on page 139. Trace the design on to the centre of the fabric (see page 14 for more information on how to effectively trace your designs on to the fabric).

4 Evenly stretch the fabric on to the hoop (see page 15 for further instructions) so that the design is central in the hoop.

5 You will punch the shapes working outwards from the centre. Thread your needle with one of the colours for a semi-circle and start there.

6 Punch the outline of the shape, punching in every other hole, then fill in punching in every third hole (see page 19 for more information on how to punch with the regular needle).

7 Continue to punch in this manner for the rest of the shapes.

8 Once all of the shapes are punched, move on to the background.

9 Punch the border of the pendant first, punch in every other hole and punch two rows close together. With the border punched, now start on the background. The outline stitches are all in place so you can fill in all of the background, punching in roughly every third hole.

To finish the pendant hanging

1 The pendant will be hung using a piece of dowel and yarn at the top. It is finished with a small hem on the back.

2 Using a fine paintbrush and PVA glue, paint a line of glue ¾in (2cm) away from the finished piece to create a border and allow to dry. Paint this line at least ¼in (0.5cm) thick along the curved edge. You will need to snip into this edge to ensure it doesn't pucker when you hem it.

3 Once dry, cut along the outside of the glued edge. It will stop the fabric from fraying.

4 Snip into the outline at roughly ⅜in (1cm) intervals along the curved edge.

5 Pin and stitch the hem in place.

6 Decide which colour yarn you would like to use to attach the dowel to the pendant and cut a piece that is 59in (150cm) in length.

7 Thread the yarn on to a darning needle, insert into the hem at the top of the pendant and knot.

8 Using a whip-stitch, attach the dowel to the top of the pendant with the yarn. Stitch the yarn over the dowel three times at each end and knot, leaving the middle part of the dowel exposed.

9 Next, cut a piece of yarn to hang your pendant. This will need to be 15¾in (40 cm) in length (or you can make it longer or shorter depending on how far you would like it to hang). Attach this at either end of the dowel and your pendant is ready to hang.

Tip

Why not make another in a slightly different size with coordinating colours?

HANGING HEART DECORATION

Spread the love around your home with this decorative yet simple hanging heart. It's filled with a small amount of polyester filling that could be changed for dried lavender for an aromatic alternative.

SKILL LEVEL: EASY

YOU'LL NEED:

- Frame for stretching the fabric – I used a 7in (17.5cm) no-slip hoop

- Monk's cloth fabric – 9½in (24cm) square

- Approximately 70g of bulky-weight yarn (CYC group 5)

- #10 Oxford regular punch needle

- Fabric scissors

- Embroidery scissors or snips

- Sewing needle and matching thread

- Tape measure

- Small amount of recycled polyester toy filling

STATIONERY:

- Masking tape

- Permanent marker or pencil

- Plain paper

- PVA (or alternative strong glue) and fine paintbrush

OPTIONAL:

- Lightbox

HANGING HEART DECORATION

Size: The pattern will make one hanging heart decoration measuring approximately 4in (10cm).

ABOUT THE PROJECT

The looped stitches are visible on both sides of the hanging decoration. The heart is filled with recycled polyester toy filling.

METHOD

To punch the hanging heart decoration
The heart is double-sided so you will need to punch two matching hearts, then sew them together.

1 Measure and cut 2 x 9½in (24cm) square pieces of monk's cloth.

2 Tape the edges of the fabric with masking tape so the fabric does not fray. Alternatively, you can overlock the edges if you prefer.

3 The template for the motif can be found on page 129. Trace the heart design on to the centre of each piece of fabric (see page 14 for more information on how to effectively trace your designs on to the fabric).

4 Evenly stretch the fabric on to the hoop (see page 15 for further instructions) so that the design is central in the hoop.

5 The heart is punched in one colour so you will start with the outline and then fill in.

6 Thread your needle with your yarn and punch in every other hole along the outline of the heart. This will help to give your outline some definition (see page 19 for more information on outlining with the regular needle).

7 Once outlined, fill in the heart, punching in every third hole (see page 19 for more information on how to fill in with the regular needle).

8 Once you have finished punching, remove from the hoop and punch the second heart.

9 When you have finished punching both hearts, snip any yarn ends that may be protruding. As the hearts are one solid colour you will not need to tidy or poke any stitches into place.

To sew up the hanging heart decoration

It is easiest to complete the sewing by hand.

1 As the heart is quite small it will probably not require any steaming, but if it is does, a light steam will probably be all that is required (see the instructions on steaming on page 23).

2 Once you have finished punching, use your fine paintbrush to paint a line of glue approximately ⅜in (1cm) away from the finished edge. You will want to paint this line quite thick, about ¼in (0.5cm), as you will need to snip into this once dry to help with puckering. Allow to dry according to the instructions on the glue.

3 Once dry, cut your heart along the outside of the glued edge. It will stop the fabric from fraying.

4 Snip into the outline at roughly ⅜in (1cm) intervals all the way round. This will help to stop any puckering when stitching the two hearts together. Complete this for both hearts.

5 Place the two hearts together with the right sides facing outwards.

6 Tuck the hems inside into the cavity of the heart.

7 Pin the two pieces together, leaving the top two arches open at this point.

8 Thread your needle with a thread in a similar colour to your yarn.

9 Stitch the heart together along the two long sides that you have pinned, using small whip-stitches.

10 Pin one of the arches together at the top of the heart and stitch together.

11 Now fill your heart with the stuffing.

12 Stitch the other arch together. As you reach the point where the two arches meet, pause.

13 Cut a 7¾in (20cm) piece of yarn and fold it over so the ends are together.

14 Push the ends approximately ¾in (2cm) into the small opening where the two arches meet.

15 Pinch this in place as you complete the remainder of the stitches, stitching this piece of yarn into the heart. Stitch over this part a few times to strengthen.

16 You can use this yarn loop to hang your decoration.

Tip

Why not put something scented in with your filling and then use the hanging decoration in a wardrobe or closet to keep your clothes smelling fresh?

COASTERS

You won't find coasters this stunning in the shops. Co-ordinate them with your room scheme using different coloured yarns. Alternatively, use up your oddments and make an eclectic assortment ideal for craft fairs and charity sales.

SKILL LEVEL: EASY

YOU'LL NEED:

- Frame for stretching the fabric –
  I used a 7in (17.5cm) no-slip hoop

- Monk's cloth fabric –
  four x 7¾in (20cm) square pieces

- Approximately 70g medium-weight yarn (CYC group 4)

- #14 Oxford fine punch needle

- Fabric scissors

- Embroidery scissors or snips

- Sewing needle and matching thread

- Tape measure

STATIONERY:

- Masking tape

- Permanent marker or pencil

- Plain paper

- PVA (or alternative strong glue) and fine paintbrush

OPTIONAL:

- Lightbox

COASTERS

Size: Each coaster measures 4in (10cm) square once punched.

ABOUT THE PROJECT

The looped stitches are visible on the finished side of the coasters, with a small hem underneath to finish off the fabric.

METHOD

To punch the coasters

1 Measure and cut a 7¾in (20cm) square piece of monk's cloth.

2 Tape the edges of the fabric with masking tape so the fabric does not fray. Alternatively, you can overlock the edges if you prefer.

3 Leaving at least a 2in (5cm) border of monk's cloth for stretching on to the hoop, draw out a 7½in (9cm) square on the monk's cloth (see page 14 on how to draw).

4 The templates for the motifs can be found on page 130. Choose which one of the four coasters you are going to punch first and trace the design from the book on to a piece of A4 paper (see page 14 for more information on tracing a pattern) using a pencil. Alternatively, trace them all in one go.

5 Go over the pencil outline with a permanent marker pen.

6 If you are using a window as your light source, tape the design on to the window.

7 Hold your monk's cloth over the paper on the window and using a permanent marker, trace the design on to the monk's cloth within the square you have drawn.

8 Evenly stretch the fabric on to the hoop (see page 15 for further instructions) so that the design is in the middle of the hoop.

9 Whichever coaster you decide to start with, you will need to punch the border first.

10 Thread your fine punch needle in the first border colour.

To finish the coasters

1 The coasters will be finished using a small hem so that they will sit flat and not be too bulky.

2 If you have used rug yarn to punch your coasters, you may want to give them a light steam before hemming (see the instructions on steaming on page 23).

3 Once you have finished punching, use your fine paintbrush to paint a line of glue approximately ⅜in (1cm) away from the finished punching edge. Allow this to dry according to the instructions on the glue.

4 Once dry, cut your coasters along this glued edge. It will stop the fabric from fraying (see the instructions on gluing on page 23).

5 Finish the coasters with a ⅜in (1cm) hem (following the hemming instructions on page 24).

Tips

Steaming the coasters when you have finished punching (but before finishing) will help the loops to sit a little flatter and ensure glasses don't wobble. Place your punched piece with the loop side up on an ironing board. Set the iron to a setting that does not produce steam. Wet a hand towel with cold water and place over the punched piece. Press and hold the iron on the wet towel to create its own steam. Hold for 10-15 seconds, then move to the next area.

When punching the eyes of the fish, make sure you punch into the fabric a minimum of three times.

11 Punch in every hole along the border outline you have drawn, changing colour where necessary.

12 Punch a second row directly inside the first border row. These two outside rows, close together, will ensure there aren't any gaps once your coaster is hemmed.

13 For the rest of the punching you will punch leaving a gap in between rows (see page 19 for more information on punching with a fine needle).

14 When punching one of the coasters with a fish head, start with the eye. Make three punches with your needle close together in a triangle shape.

15 Once punched, push both tails through to the looped side. It won't look like an eye immediately, but once you've got other stitches surrounding it, the shape will be visible.

16 Move on to the outline of the shapes, punching in every hole for a crisp line.

17 With the outlines punched, move on to filling in the rest of the shapes (see page 20 for more information on punching with a fine needle).

18 Once in the centre of the shape, pull the punch needle up to expose ⅜in (1cm) of yarn.

19 Cut the yarn off and using the closed, pointed end of embroidery scissors, push the small piece of yarn through to the loopy side.

20 Continue punching all of the shapes.

21 Once all punched, change your yarn to the next colour and punch the remaining parts.

22 When all of the shapes are punched, punch the background.

TRIVET

Put some citrus style and strong texture into your kitchen or on your dining table with this practical hot pan trivet. With an eye-catching lemon motif, it's bound to get dinner conversations flowing.

SKILL LEVEL: MOVING ON

YOU'LL NEED:

- Frame for stretching the fabric – I used a 9in (23cm) no-slip hoop

- Monk's cloth fabric – 13in (33cm) square

- Approximately 70g of medium-weight yarn (CYC group 4)

- #14 Oxford fine punch needle

- Fabric scissors

- Embroidery scissors or snips

- Yarn needle

- Tape measure

STATIONERY:

- Masking tape

- Permanent marker or pencil

- Plain paper

- Pegs or small clips

OPTIONAL:

- Lightbox

TRIVET

Size: The trivet will be a 7¾in (20cm) circle once finished.

ABOUT THE PROJECT

The looped stitches are visible on the finished side of the trivet, with no hem as the edges are whipped for a neat finish.

METHOD

To punch the trivet

1 Measure and cut a 13in (33cm) square piece of monk's cloth.

2 Tape the edges of the fabric with masking tape so the fabric does not fray whilst you are punching.

3 The template for the motif can be found on page 131 and needs to be copied at 111%. Trace your design on to the fabric in the centre (see page 14 for more information on tracing on to the fabric).

4 Evenly stretch the fabric on to the hoop (see page 15 for further instructions) so that the design is in the middle of the hoop.

5 Starting in the centre of the design, punch the outline of the leaves.

6 Fill in the leaves whilst your needle is still threaded with the green. Punch in every hole and leave a gap in between rows (see page 20 for more information on punching with a fine needle).

7 Next, thread your needle with the yellow yarn and punch the lemons, using the same method as the leaves.

8 Working your way outwards, next thread your needle with the light grey yarn. Punch the outline of this organic shape, punching in every hole for definition. At the end of the outline, snip your yarn and end.

9 Using the grey, follow the shape of the leaves and lemons and outline them.

To finish the trivet

The trivet will be finished with a whipped edge to give it a neat finish and to reinforce the edges.

1 Remove the trivet from the hoop and give it a light steam to flatten it out (see page 23 for more information on steaming).

2 Trim the corners of the fabric, then roughly cut the remaining fabric so that you are left with a 2in (5cm) border of fabric around the finished punching.

3 Whip-stitch around the edge of your punching in a colour of your choosing (see page 25 for more information on whipping). You can either continue on with the background colour or choose one of the contrasting colours.

10 With these two lines of grey punching now in place, fill in the remainder of the grey area, leaving a gap between rows.

11 When all of the shapes are punched, punch the background.

12 Snip any ends in line with the loops.

13 Tidy up your punching if necessary (see page 21 for more information on tidying up).

NAPKIN HOLDERS

Stylish rings to neaten your napkins — co-ordinate them with your dining room scheme to create a chic look. They're ideal for beginners and perfect for practising your newly acquired skill.

SKILL LEVEL: EASY

YOU'LL NEED:

- Frame for stretching the fabric — I used a 10in (25.5cm) no-slip hoop

- Monk's cloth fabric — 11¾in (30cm)

- Approximately 25g of medium-weight yarn (CYC group 4)

- #14 Oxford fine punch needle

- Fabric scissors

- Embroidery scissors or snips

- Sewing needle and matching thread

- Tape measure

STATIONERY:

- Masking tape

- Permanent marker or pencil

- Plain paper

- PVA (or alternative strong glue) and fine paintbrush

OPTIONAL:

- Lightbox

NAPKIN HOLDERS

Size: The pattern will make two napkin holders, which will be 5½in (14cm) in length, 1½in (4cm) in width, with approximately 1¾in (4.5cm) wide diameter when stitched.

ABOUT THE PROJECT

The looped stitches are visible on the outside of the napkin holders and form the right side. There is a small hem underneath to finish off the fabric, with the ends stitched together to form a tube.

METHOD

To punch the napkin holders

1 Measure and cut an 11¾in (30cm) square piece of monk's cloth.

2 Tape the edges of the fabric with masking tape so the fabric does not fray. Alternatively, you can overlock the edges if you prefer.

3 The design for the napkin holders is a rectangle. The template for the motif can be found on page 130. Trace the napkin holder design twice on to the fabric, ensuring there is a gap of 2¼in (6cm) in between the two rectangles. Draw the design on to the centre of the fabric (see page 14 for more information on how to effectively trace your designs on to the fabric).

4 Evenly stretch the fabric onto the hoop (see page 15 for further instructions) so that the designs are central in the hoop.

5 The napkin holders are punched using two colours here, but you could always incorporate more.

6 Start by punching the leaf shapes and thread your fine punch needle in that colour.

7 Punch in every hole along the outline of the leaves.

8 Once you have outlined all of the leaves, fill them in, leaving a gap in between rows.

9 Punch the border of each napkin holder. Where the design meets one of the leaf shapes, continue your punching around it.

10 Once you have punched the outline in your background colour, fill in the background leaving a gap in between rows (see page 20 for more information on punching with a fine needle).

To finish the napkin holders

The napkin holders will be finished using a small hem on the inside, then stitched to form a tube.

1 As the napkin holders are small, they shouldn't curl up too much when punched. If you do find that they curl a little when you take them off the hoop, you can give them a light steam before hemming (see the instructions on steaming on page 23).

2 Once you have finished punching, use your fine paintbrush to paint a line of glue approximately ⅜in (1cm) away from the finished edge. Allow this to dry according to the instructions on the glue.

3 Once dry, cut your napkin holders along this glued edge to stop the fabric from fraying.

4 Hem the napkin holders with a ⅜in (1cm) hem (following the hemming instructions on page 24).

5 Now that the holders are hemmed you need to stitch the short ends together to form the tube. It is easier to do this with the wrong sides together.

6 With the short ends together and the loops (right side) facing outwards, use a neutral thread and needle to stitch the ends together.

Tip

This is a quick and easy project. Although the pattern is designed to make two, you could easily make four or six. Why not try inverting the colours so that the holders are a little different?

BOOKMARK

A simple colour-block bookmark is the perfect project for beginners – so easy you'll be whipping them up as gifts for family and friends. Make them in colours you know they like for that extra special touch.

SKILL LEVEL: EASY

YOU'LL NEED:

- Frame for stretching the fabric – I used a 7in (17.5cm) no-slip hoop

- Monk's cloth fabric – 9¾in (25cm) square (see tip page 89)

- Approximately 15g of medium-weight yarn (CYC group 4)

- #14 Oxford fine punch needle

- Fabric scissors

- Embroidery scissors or snips

- Sewing needle and matching thread

- Tape measure

STATIONERY:

- Masking tape

- Permanent marker or pencil

- Plain paper

- PVA (or alternative strong glue) and fine paintbrush

OPTIONAL:

- Lightbox

BOOKMARK

Size: The bookmark will be 9½in (24cm) long and 1¼in (3cm) wide once punched.

ABOUT THE PROJECT

The looped stitches are visible on the finished side of the bookmark, with a small hem underneath to finish off the fabric.

METHOD

To punch the bookmark

1 Measure and cut a 9¾in × 11¾in (25cm × 30cm) piece of monk's cloth.

2 Tape the edges of the fabric with masking tape so the fabric does not fray. Alternatively, you can overlock the edges if you prefer.

3 The template for the motif can be found on page 131 and needs to be copied at 111%. Trace the design from the book on to a plain piece of A4 paper using a pencil and then go over the pencil outline with a permanent marker pen.

4 Using a light source for tracing, lay the fabric on top of the design and trace the bookmark on, leaving a 2in (5cm) border.

5 Evenly stretch the fabric on to the hoop (see page 15 for further instructions) so that the design is in the middle of the hoop.

6 Thread your fine punch needle in the first border colour.

7 Punch in every hole along the border outline you have drawn, changing colour where necessary.

8 Punch a second row directly inside the first border row. These two outside rows, close together, will ensure there aren't any gaps once your bookmark is hemmed and will allow it to lie flat.

9 For the rest of the punching you will punch leaving a gap in between rows (see page 20 for more information on punching with a fine needle).

10 Move on to the outline of the shapes, punching in every hole for a crisp line.

To finish the bookmark

1 The bookmark will be finished using a small hem so that it will sit flatter on the page.

2 As the bookmark is small it shouldn't curl up too much when punched. If you do find when you take it off the hoop that it is curling, you can give it a light steam before hemming (see the instructions on steaming on page 23).

3 Once you have finished punching, use your fine paintbrush to paint a line of glue approximately ⅜in (1cm) away from the finished edge. Allow this to dry (according to the instructions on the glue).

4 Once dry, cut your bookmark along this glued edge. It will stop the fabric from fraying.

5 Hem the bookmark with a ⅜in (1cm) hem (following the hemming instructions on page 24).

11 With the outlines punched, move on to filling in the rest of the shape, punching in every other hole, leaving a gap between rows.

12 Once in the centre of the shape, pull the punch needle up to expose ⅜in (1cm) of yarn.

13 Cut the yarn off and using the closed, pointed end of embroidery scissors, push the small piece of yarn through to the loopy side.

14 Continue punching all of the shapes.

15 Once they have all been punched, change your yarn to the next colour and punch the remaining parts.

Tips

You'll find that when you draw your bookmark on to the fabric there is extra space (due to the width needed to fit in the hoop), so why not draw another bookmark on so you have a spare! If drawing two bookmarks on, leave a 2in (5cm) gap in between.

This bookmark requires hardly any yarn to make – why not use up some scraps?

Why not make different sized bookmarks to fit in different books? They make a great present for a friend that loves to read.

CELESTIAL HOOP ART

Less really is more with this minimal design – use a simple sun and moon motif to create an attractive picture. The beautiful chalky shades bring a modern touch to this much-loved subject and offer a contemporary look to the fascination that we have with the sky.

SKILL LEVEL: EASY

YOU'LL NEED:

- 7in (17.5cm) embroidery hoop

- Monk's cloth fabric – 13½in (34cm) square

- Approximately 40g of medium-weight yarn (CYC group 4)

- #14 Oxford fine punch needle

- Fabric scissors

- Embroidery scissors or snips

- Darning needle

- Tape measure

- Dylon All-in-1 fabric dye (smoke grey)

STATIONERY:

- Card

- Paper scissors

- White permanent marker or dressmaker's / tailor's chalk

- PVA (or alternative strong glue) and fine paintbrush

CELESTIAL HOOP ART

Size: The wall hanging will be made using a 7in (17.5cm) embroidery hoop and this will be the finished size.

ABOUT THE PROJECT

The flat stitches will be visible on the finished side of the hoop, with part of the dyed fabric left exposed as the background.

METHOD

To punch the wall hanging

Unlike some of the other projects where you will work in a frame or hoop, remove your project and finish it in another way, this wall hanging will be made in the embroidery hoop and then remain there for finishing.

1 Measure and cut a 13½in (34cm) square piece of monk's cloth. This is a larger piece of fabric than you would normally need, as you will be dyeing the fabric and it may shrink a little in the wash.

2 You do not need to do anything to secure the edges of the fabric, as you will be gluing it to the hoop.

3 According to the instructions on the dye, dye your fabric and allow it to dry.

4 Follow the instructions on pages 14–22 Getting Started tips and tricks – punching into an embroidery hoop – to stretch and glue your fabric into the hoop.

5 You will be punching on to the front of the hoop, so that the flat stitches are visible. They help to give definition and a neat finish to the design.

6 The template for the motif can be found on page 140. As the fabric is now a dark grey, you will be unable to trace your design as you may have done in other projects. Instead, once you have traced your design from the book, copy it on to a piece of card and cut out the sun and moon shapes from the card.

7 Using a white permanent marker pen or tailor's chalk, trace the design on to the centre of the hoop. You will be tracing your design on to the front or finished side of the hoop, as you will be punching from the finished side to create flat stitches.

8 For the sun's rays, draw short ¾in (2cm) lines extending from the sun, ensuring that there is still a small gap of fabric before the edge of the hoop.

9 With your design drawn on, thread your needle with your yarn and punch the sun and moon shapes, start with the outline first and then fill in. You will want to keep your stitches as close as possible and ensure that all of the fabric is covered (see page 19 for more information on different stitches).

10 When you have finished punching, turn over the hoop and snip off all of the ends flush with the loops.

11 As the flat stitches are visible on the front you will not need to do any tidying up of stitches.

TABLET COVER

Get tech-savvy and keep your tablet safe and protected when out and about with this stylish tablet cosy – its bold chevron patterning will make a smart and practical addition to your handbag and the loopy textured fabric helps to protect your device. Team with the Laptop Pouch (see page 114) and create a coordinating set.

SKILL LEVEL: EASY

YOU'LL NEED:

- Frame for stretching the fabric – I used a 16in (40.5cm) canvas stretcher bar frame

- Monk's cloth fabric – 19¾in (50cm) square

- Approximately 130g of bulky-weight yarn (CYC group 5)

- #10 Oxford regular punch needle

- Fabric scissors

- Embroidery scissors or snips

- Sewing needle and matching thread

- Tape measure

- One piece of backing fabric, I used a wool mix felt (only cut this once you have finished punching), no larger than 7½ x 10¼in (19 x 26cm)

STATIONERY:

- Masking tape

- Permanent marker or pencil

- Plain paper

- PVA (or alternative strong glue) and fine paintbrush

OPTIONAL:

- Lightbox

- Sewing machine

TABLET COVER

Size: The pattern will make one tablet cover that is approximately 7 x 9¾in (18 x 25cm) when punched. If you are unsure if this will fit your tablet, measure yours before you start and adjust the sizing accordingly.

ABOUT THE PROJECT

The looped stitches are visible on the outside of the tablet cover and form the right side. There is a small hem underneath to finish off the fabric, with a wool mix felt used for the back of the pouch.

METHOD

To punch the tablet cover

1 Measure and cut a 19¾in (50cm) square piece of monk's cloth.

2 Tape the edges of the fabric with masking tape so the fabric does not fray. Alternatively, you can overlock the edges if you prefer.

3 The template for the motif can be found on page 134. Trace the design on to the fabric. You can use a ruler if you are struggling to trace the diagonal lines (see page 14 for more information on how to effectively trace your designs on to the fabric).

4 Evenly stretch the fabric on to the frame (see page 14 for further instructions) so that the designs are central in the frame.

5 All of the diagonal shapes are similar in that they touch other shapes and form part of the border, so you can punch them in any order – apart from the finger loops in the cream section, which you should leave until last.

6 Thread your needle with the first colour and punch the outline of your shape, punching in every other hole. Once you have punched the outline, continue on the same shape and fill in, punching in roughly every third hole.

7 Continue in this manner until all of the shapes have been punched (see page 19 for more information on how to punch with the regular needle).

To finish the tablet cover

The tablet cover will be finished with a backing fabric to form the pouch for the tablet to slot into.

1 The tablet cover may require steaming before you attach the back (see the instructions on steaming on page 23).

2 Once you have finished punching, use your fine paintbrush to paint a line of glue approximately ½in (1.5 cm) away from the finished edge. Allow this to dry according to the instructions on the glue.

3 Once dry, cut your tablet cover along this glued edge. It will stop the fabric from fraying.

8 For the cream section with the finger loops, punch the outline of the shape, punching in every other hole. Then for two rows within the shape, create finger loops that are approximately 1in (2cm) tall (see page 19 for more information on finger loops).

4 Measure the punched piece including the monk's cloth border and cut a piece of backing fabric the same size, e.g. if your punched piece has not grown it will still measure 9¾ x 7in (24.5 x 17.5cm) so the piece you will cut will be 10¾ x 8in (27.5 x 20.5cm). I used wool mix felt as it does not fray and so does not require hemming before use. It's a nice, easy fabric to sew with as a beginner.

5 First you will need to sew a small hem on to one long edge of the backing fabric.

6 Fold one long edge over ⅜in (1cm), pin and sew a straight line of stitching.

7 Place the backing fabric on the table with the right side facing up.

8 Place the punched piece on to the fabric with the right side (loop stitches) facing downwards.

9 Pin the two pieces together.

10 Thread your needle with a thread in a similar colour to your backing material.

11 Sew three of the sides together, the two shorter sides and the bottom edge (the long edge without a hem). If using a sewing machine to stitch together, use a zipper foot so that you can sew as close as possible all the way around the cover edge. If stitching by hand you'll be able to get pretty close.

12 Remove the pins and turn right side out.

CARD HOLDER

Keep all your essential cards safely in one place and always to hand in this attractive and useful holder. The sewing up makes it the ideal project if you're looking to step up a level, and is well worth the effort.

SKILL LEVEL: MOVING ON

YOU'LL NEED:

- Frame for stretching the fabric – I used a 7in (17.5cm) Morgan no-slip hoop

- Monk's cloth fabric – 9½in (24cm) square

- Approximately 20g of medium-weight yarn (CYC group 4)

- #14 Oxford fine punch needle

- Fabric scissors

- Embroidery scissors or snips

- Sewing needle and matching thread

- Tape measure

- One small piece of lining fabric. I used a wool mix felt (only cut this once you have finished punching), no larger than 5½in x 3⅛in (14 x 8cm)

STATIONERY:

- Masking tape

- Permanent marker or pencil

- Plain paper

- PVA (or alternative strong glue) and fine paintbrush

OPTIONAL:

- Lightbox

CARD HOLDER

Size: The pattern will make one card holder, which will fit two to three bank cards in.

ABOUT THE PROJECT

The looped stitches are visible on the outside of the card holder, which is then lined to create the enclosure for the cards.

METHOD

To punch the card holder

1 Measure and cut a 9½in (24cm) square piece of monk's cloth.

2 Tape the edges of the fabric with masking tape so the fabric does not fray. Alternatively, you can overlock the edges if you prefer.

3 The design for the card holder is a rectangle.

4 Draw a 3¾ x 2¾in (9.5 x 7cm) rectangle on to the centre of the fabric.

5 The template for the motif can be found on page 128. Trace the design on to the fabric, ensuring it is in the centre of the fabric (see page 14 for more information on how to effectively trace your designs on to the fabric).

6 Evenly stretch the fabric on to the hoop (see page 15 for further instructions on stretching the fabric) so that the design is central in the hoop.

7 You will be using the same stitch with the fine needle, punching in every hole (see page 20 for more information on punching with a fine needle).

8 All of the geometric shapes are similar in that they touch other shapes and form part of the border, so you can punch them in any order.

9 Thread your needle with the first colour and start punching the outline of one of the shapes, then fill in. Punch two rows together and then leave a gap. Continue in this pattern for the rest of the punching.

10 Punch all three shapes in this manner.

11 Once you have finished punching, snip any ends and push them through to the loopy side. Snip any ends off flush with the loops.

To finish the card holder

The card holder is finished with a small hem, then it is lined to create the pouch for the cards to sit in.

1 As the card holder is very small, it shouldn't curl up too much when punched and won't require steaming.

2 Once you have finished punching, use your fine paintbrush to paint a line of glue approximately ⅜in (1cm) away from the finished edge. Allow this to dry according to the instructions on the glue.

3 Once dry, cut your card holder along this glued edge. It will stop the fabric from fraying.

4 Hem the card holder with a ⅜in (1cm) hem (following the hemming instructions on page 24).

5 With the holder now punched and hemmed, lay it flat on the table with the wrong side (flat stitches with hem) facing upwards.

6 Measure the card holder from the outer edges of the hemmed monk's cloth. Your cover may have grown a little during punching. Using this new measurement, add 1½in (4cm) to the shortest measurement to find the size you need for your lining fabric, e.g. if your card holder hasn't grown and still measures 3¾ x 2¾in (9.5 x 7cm), you will need to cut a piece that is 3¾ x 4¼in (9.5 x 11cm). This extra fabric will give you the pouch on one end to slot the cards into. I used a wool mix felt as it doesn't require hemming.

7 Cut out your rectangle of lining fabric.

8 Lay the punched piece on the table with the flat stitches and hem facing up. Place the lining fabric on top of this and make sure the extra 1½in (4cm) of fabric hangs over one end. The three other sides should all line up with the monk's cloth.

9 Pin the three sides which line up together.

10 Using a needle and thread in a similar colour to your lining fabric, use small whip-stitches to attach the lining fabric to the holder along each of the three pinned sides.

11 With the three sides all stitched together, fold the extra 1½in (4cm) fabric back on to the lining and pin in place. This extra piece will form the slot for the cards to sit in.

12 Leaving the inner edge of the fabric flap open, pin the two sides.

13 Using a needle and thread, use small whip-stitches to stitch the two sides to the lining fabric underneath.

14 Once the lining fabric has been attached to the punched piece it is complete. You can now slide your cards in.

SUNGLASSES CASE

An ultra-cool case to store your eyewear, which you could easily find in an expensive gift shop – only you can make this one yourself. The soft punched fabric creates a cushioned effect to keep your reading or sunglasses from being scratched.

SKILL LEVEL: EASY

YOU'LL NEED:

- Frame for stretching the fabric – I used a 10in (25.5cm) no-slip hoop

- Monk's cloth fabric – 11¾in (30cm) square

- Approximately 60g of medium-weight yarn (CYC group 4)

- #14 Oxford fine punch needle

- Fabric scissors

- Embroidery scissors or snips

- Sewing needle and matching thread

- Tape measure

STATIONERY:

- Masking tape

- Permanent marker or pencil

- Plain paper

- PVA (or alternative strong glue) and fine paintbrush

OPTIONAL:

- Lightbox

SUNGLASSES CASE

Size: The pattern will make a sunglasses case, which will measure 6¼in x 4in (16 x 10cm) when sewn up.

ABOUT THE PROJECT

The looped stitches are visible on the outside of the sunglasses case.

METHOD

To punch the sunglasses case

1 Measure and cut an 11¾in (30cm) square piece of monk's cloth.

2 Tape the edges of the fabric with masking tape so the fabric does not fray. Alternatively, you can overlock the edges if you prefer.

3 The design for the sunglasses case is a rectangle.

4 Draw a 7¾in x 6¼in (20 x 16cm) rectangle on to the centre of the fabric.

5 The template for the motif can be found on page 132. Trace the design on to the fabric, ensuring it is in the centre of the fabric (see page 14 for more information on how to effectively trace your designs on to the fabric).

6 Evenly stretch the fabric on to the hoop (see page 15 for further instructions) so that the design is central in the hoop.

7 You will be using the same stitch with the fine needle, punching in every hole (see page 20 for more information on punching with a fine needle).

8 Start by punching the outline of the semi-circle and then fill in. Punch two rows together and then leave a gap.

9 Once the semi-circle is punched, punch the background in the same way.

10 Once you have finished punching, snip any ends and push them through to the loopy side. Snip any ends off flush with the loops.

To finish the sunglasses case

The sunglasses case is finished with a small hem, then it is sewn together to form a pouch for the glasses to slide into.

1 As the sunglasses cover is small it shouldn't curl up too much when punched. If you do find that it is curled when you remove it from the hoop, you can give it a light steam before hemming (see the instructions on steaming on page 23).

2 Once you have finished punching, use your fine paintbrush to paint a line of glue approximately ⅜in (1cm) away from the finished edge. Allow this to dry according to the instructions on the glue.

3 Once dry, cut your sunglasses case along this glued edge. It will stop the fabric from fraying.

4 Hem the sunglasses case with a ⅜in (1cm) hem (following the hemming instructions on page 24).

5 With the case now punched, lay it flat on the table with the wrong side (flat stitches with hem) facing upwards.

6 With the wrong sides together (the flat stitches and the side with the hem) fold the punched piece in half so that it now measures approximately 6¼in x 4in (16 x 10cm).

7 Pin the long edge together and one of the shorter edges.

8 Using a needle and thread in a similar colour to the yarn, make small whip-stitches to sew the edges together.

9 With two edges now sewn together your case is complete.

> *Tip*
>
> If you want to line the sunglasses case for extra protection, cut a piece of fabric the same size as your finished piece of punching and stitch it to the wrong side before sewing the edges together.

PASSPORT COVER

Add some creative style to your hand luggage with a beautiful travel cover for your passport. Make it in colours to match your suitcases for a totally co-ordinated look.

SKILL LEVEL: MOVING ON

YOU'LL NEED:

- Frame for stretching the fabric –
  I used a 10in (25.5cm) no-slip hoop

- Monk's cloth fabric –
  11¾in (30cm) square

- Approximately 50g of medium-weight yarn (CYC group 4)

- #14 Oxford fine punch needle

- Fabric scissors

- Embroidery scissors or snips

- Sewing needle and matching thread

- Tape measure

- One small piece of lining fabric.
  I used a wool mix felt (only cut this
  once you have finished punching),
  no larger than 6in x 11¾in
  (15 x 30cm)

STATIONERY:

- Masking tape

- Permanent marker or pencil

- Plain paper

- PVA (or alternative strong glue)
  and fine paintbrush

OPTIONAL:

- Lightbox

PASSPORT COVER

Size: The pattern will make one passport cover, which will fit snuggly over a European passport, which is 5 x 3½in (12.5 x 9cm) when closed.

ABOUT THE PROJECT

The looped stitches are visible on the outside of the passport cover, which is then lined to create the enclosure for the passport.

METHOD

To punch the passport cover

1 Measure and cut a 11¾in (30cm) square piece of monk's cloth.

2 Tape the edges of the fabric with masking tape so the fabric does not fray. Alternatively, you can overlock the edges if you prefer.

3 The design for the passport cover is a rectangle.

4 Draw a 7¼in x 5¼in (18.5 x 13.5cm) rectangle on to the centre of the fabric.

5 The template for the motif can be found on page 133. Trace the design on to the fabric, ensuring it is in the centre (see page 14 for more information on how to effectively trace your designs on to the fabric).

6 Evenly stretch the fabric onto the hoop (see page 15 for further instructions) so that the design is central in the hoop.

7 You will be using the same stitch with the fine needle, punching in every hole (see page 20 for more information on punching with a fine needle).

8 Start with punching the outline of the semi-circle and then fill in. Punch two rows together and then leave a gap.

9 Once the semi-circle is punched, then punch the background in the same way.

10 Once you have finished punching, snip any ends and push them through to the loopy side. Snip any ends off flush with the loops.

To finish the passport cover

The passport cover is finished with a small hem, then it is lined to create the pouch for the passport to sit in.

1 As the passport cover is small, it shouldn't curl up too much when punched. If you do find that it curls when you remove it from the hoop, you can give it a light steam before hemming (see the instructions on steaming on page 23).

2 Once you have finished punching, use your fine paintbrush to paint a line of glue approximately ⅜in (1cm) away from the finished edge. Allow this to dry according to the instructions on the glue.

3 Once dry, cut your passport cover along this glued edge. It will stop the fabric from fraying.

4 Hem the passport cover with a ⅜in (1cm) hem (following the hemming instructions on page 24).

5 With the cover now punched, lay it flat on the table with the wrong side (flat stitches with hem) facing upwards.

6 Measure the passport cover from the outer edges of the hemmed monk's cloth. Your cover may have grown a little during punching. Using this new measurement, add 4in (10cm) to the longest measurement to find the size you need for your lining fabric, e.g. if your passport cover hasn't grown and still measures 7¼ x 5¼in (18.5 x 13.5cm), you will need to cut a piece that is 11¼ x 5¼in (28.5 x 13.5cm). This extra fabric will give you the pouch either end to slide the passport cover into. I used a wool mix felt as it doesn't require hemming. Cut out your lining fabric.

7 Lay the punched piece on the table with the flat stitches and hem facing up. Place the lining fabric on top of this and make sure the extra fabric at each end is equal (approximately 2in (5cm) at each end).

8 Pin the two pieces together.

9 Using a needle and thread in a similar colour to your lining fabric, use small whip-stitches to attach the lining fabric to the passport along each long side.

10 With the two long sides attached, fold the extra fabric back on to the lining and pin in place. These two extra pieces will form the pockets that the cover will fit into.

11 Leaving the inner edge of the fabric flap open, pin the top and bottom.

12 Using a needle and thread, use small whip-stitches to stitch the top and bottom of the flap to the lining fabric underneath.

13 Once the lining fabric has been attached to the punched piece it is complete. You can now slide your passport in.

Tip

This pattern could also work for a notebook or diary cover. Alter the measurements to fit the book.

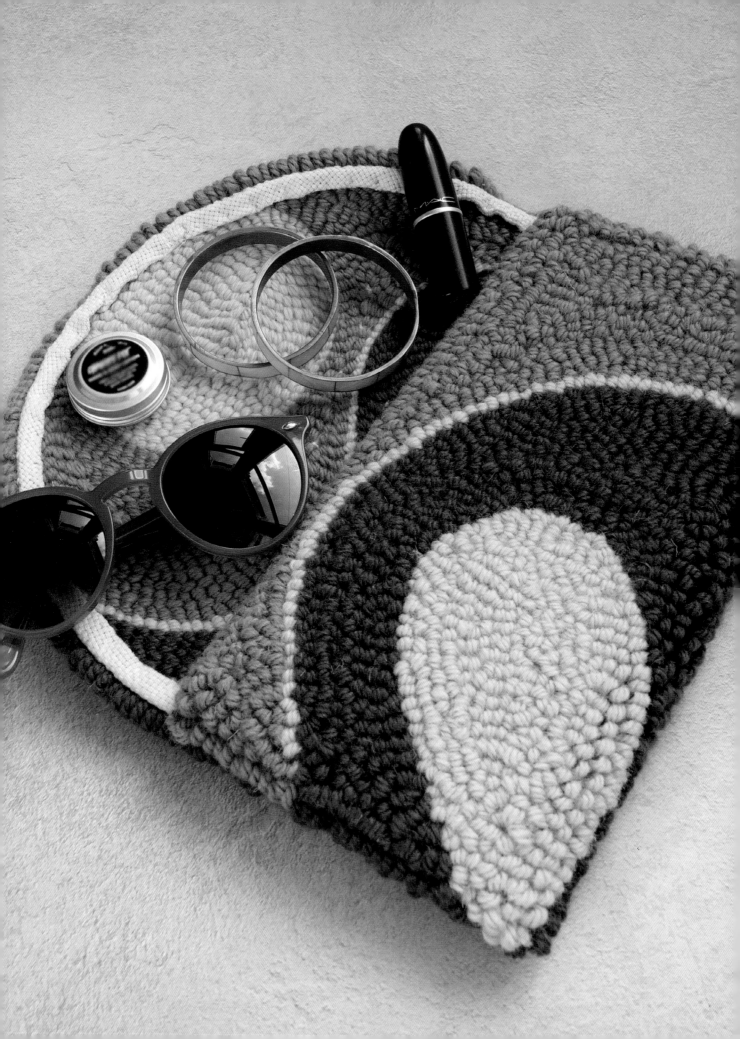

CLUTCH BAG

A neat little clutch bag to show off your skills that really is a work of art. Its compact size is just big enough for all the essentials you need on a night out.

SKILL LEVEL: MOVING ON

YOU'LL NEED:

- Frame for stretching the fabric – I used a 24in (61cm) no-slip hoop

- Monk's cloth fabric – 27½in (70cm) square

- Approximately 300g of bulky-weight yarn (CYC group 5)

- #10 Oxford regular punch needle

- Fabric scissors

- Embroidery scissors or snips

- Sewing needle and matching thread

- Tape measure

STATIONERY:

- Masking tape

- Permanent marker or pencil

- Plain paper

- PVA (or alternative strong glue) and fine paintbrush

- Clips or pegs

OPTIONAL:

- Lightbox

CLUTCH BAG

Size: The bag will be 7in (18cm) at the widest point and 7¾in (20cm) at the tallest point.

ABOUT THE PROJECT

The looped stitches are visible on the right side of the bag. The punched part is finished with a small hem. The oval edge provides the flap for closure.

METHOD

To punch the clutch bag

1 Measure and cut a 27½in (70cm) square piece of monk's cloth.

2 Tape the edges of the fabric with masking tape so the fabric does not fray. Alternatively, you can overlock the edges if you prefer.

3 The template for the motif can be found on page 138 and needs to be copied at 150%. Trace the design on to the centre of the fabric. (See page 14 for more information on how to effectively trace your designs on to the fabric.)

4 Evenly stretch the fabric on to the hoop (see page 15 for further instructions) so that the design is central in the hoop.

5 You will punch the thin, light line first before punching any of the solid shapes. Thread your needle with the yarn and punch this line, punching in every other hole to ensure a solid line of stitches.

6 Next you will punch the other shapes. When your needle is threaded with a particular colour, punch all of these shapes in one go.

7 Punch the outline of the shape, punching in every other hole, then fill in punching in every third hole. (See page 19 for more information on how to punch with the regular needle.)

8 Punch in this manner for all of the shapes.

9 Once you have finished punching, push any ends through to the right side, turn over and snip. Poke any stitches into place.

To finish the clutch bag

The bag is finished with a small hem on the back and a flap for closure. The punched piece is essentially folded into thirds to create the bag, with the top third (curved edge) being slightly shorter than the bottom two thirds which form the bag.

1 Using a fine paintbrush and PVA glue, paint a line of glue ½in (1.5cm) away from the finished piece to create a border and allow to dry. Paint this line at least ¼in (0.5cm) thick along the curved edge. You will need to snip into this edge to ensure it doesn't pucker when you hem it.

2 Once dry, cut along the outside of the glued edge. It will stop the fabric from fraying.

3 Snip into the outline at roughly ⅜in (1cm) intervals along the curved edge.

4 Pin and stitch the hem in place.

5 Fold the flat short end of the punched piece over (flat stitches together, loopy stitches facing outwards). The folded part should measure approximately 6in (15cm) tall. These two bottom thirds of the piece folded over form the bag.

6 Using clips or pegs, hold this folded part in place along the two short edges.

7 Using a needle and thread in a similar colour to your yarn, use small whip-stitches to stitch the two bottom thirds of the bag together along the short edges.

8 You can now fold over the remaining top third (with the curved edge) and this becomes the flap for the clutch.

Tip

If you want your bag to be lined, once you have hemmed your punched piece, cut a piece of fabric the same size and stitch on to the flat stitch side before folding and sewing into place.

LAPTOP POUCH

Store and protect your laptop in this stylish pouch. Its modern, abstract pattern and bold colours will sit comfortably in either a work or social setting and it pairs stylishly with the Tablet Cover (see page 94). The great thing about it is that it's not as difficult to make as you might think.

SKILL LEVEL: EASY

YOU'LL NEED:

- Frame for stretching the fabric – I used an 18in (46.5cm) canvas stretcher bar frame

- Monk's cloth fabric – 21¾in (55cm) square

- Approximately 165g of bulky-weight yarn (CYC group 5)

- #10 Oxford regular punch needle

- Fabric scissors

- Embroidery scissors or snips

- Sewing needle and matching thread

- Tape measure

- One piece of backing fabric. I used a wool mix felt (only cut this once you have finished punching), no larger than 13 x 11¼in (35 x 28cm)

STATIONERY:

- Masking tape

- Permanent marker or pencil

- Plain paper

- PVA (or alternative strong glue) and fine paintbrush

OPTIONAL:

- Lightbox

- Sewing machine

LAPTOP POUCH

Size: The pattern will make one laptop pouch that is approximately 9¾ x 13½in (25 x 34cm) when punched. If you are unsure as to whether this will fit your laptop, measure it before you start and adjust the sizing accordingly.

ABOUT THE PROJECT

The looped stitches are visible on the outside of the laptop pouch and a wool mix felt is used for the back of the pouch.

METHOD

To punch the laptop pouch

1 Measure and cut a 21¾in (55cm) square piece of monk's cloth.

2 Tape the edges of the fabric with masking tape so the fabric does not fray. Alternatively, you can overlock the edges if you prefer.

3 The template for the motif can be found on page 135 and needs to be copied at 200%. Trace the design on to the fabric (see page 14 for more information on how to effectively trace your design on to the fabric).

4 Evenly stretch the fabric on to the frame (see page 15 for further instructions) so that the design is central in the frame.

5 You will punch the semi-circle first. Thread your needle in this colour.

6 Punch in every other hole for the outline of the semi-circle, then fill in punching in every third hole (see page 19 for more information on how to punch with the regular needle).

7 Next, punch each of the larger background sections. For the outline of each of these sections, punch in every other hole for two rows, then fill in punching in every third hole.

8 Once these sections are punched you can finish with the finger loops section.

9 For the central section with the finger loops, punch the outline of the rectangle, punching in every other hole. Then for two rows within the shape, create finger loops that are approximately 1in (2.5cm) tall (see page 20 for more information on finger loops).

To finish the laptop pouch

The laptop pouch will be finished with a backing fabric to form the pouch for the tablet to slot into.

1 The laptop pouch may require steaming before you attach the back (see the instructions for steaming on page 23).

2 Once you have finished punching, use your fine paintbrush to paint a line of glue approximately ½in (1.5cm) away from the finished edge. Allow this to dry according to the instructions on the glue.

3 Once dry, cut your laptop pouch along this glued edge. It will stop the fabric from fraying.

4 Measure the punched piece including the monk's cloth border and cut a piece of backing fabric the same size, e.g. if your punched piece has not grown it will still measure 13 × 9½in (33 × 24cm) so the piece you will cut will be 14¼ × 10¾in (36 × 27cm). I used wool mix felt as it does not fray and so does not require hemming before use. It's a nice, easy fabric to sew with as a beginner.

5 First you will need to sew a small hem on to one long edge of the backing fabric.

6 Fold one long edge over ⅜in (1cm), pin and sew a straight line of stitching.

7 Place the backing fabric on the table with the right side facing up.

8 Place the punched piece with the right side (loop stitches) facing downwards on to the fabric.

9 Pin the two pieces together.

10 Thread your needle with a thread in a similar colour to your backing material.

11 Sew three of the sides together, the two shorter sides and the bottom edge (the long edge without a hem). If using a sewing machine to stitch together, use a zipper foot so that you can sew as close as possible all the way around the cover edge. If stitching by hand you'll be able to get pretty close.

12 Remove the pins and turn the right side out.

UPCYCLED CUSHION COVER

A simple line motif created on a ready-made cushion cover that won't take forever to make – worked in chalky pastel shades for a 'shabby chic' style that never seems to go out of fashion.

SKILL LEVEL: MOVING ON

YOU'LL NEED:

- Hoop for stretching the cushion cover – I used a 9in (23cm) no-slip hoop

- Lightweight, finely woven cushion cover 19¾in (50cm) square

- Approximately 20g of medium-weight wool (CYC group 4)

- #14 Oxford fine punch needle

- Embroidery scissors or snips

- Tape measure

- 19¾in (50cm) cushion insert

STATIONERY:

- Pencil

- Card

- Paper scissors

OPTIONAL:

- Iron-on fusible interfacing

UPCYCLED CUSHION COVER

Size: 19¾in (50cm) square.

ABOUT THE PROJECT

The cushion will have both flat and loopy stitches visible on the right side of the cushion, creating an interesting use of texture.

METHOD

To punch the cushion

As we are not punching the entirety of this item, we shall be using a template rather than tracing on a whole design. The template is used twice. Although this upcycle is relatively easy in terms of punching, it may be useful to have completed some of the 'easy' projects beforehand, so that you have had some practice punching before you attempt this project.

1 The template for the motif can be found on page 140. Trace the template on to a piece of card.

2 Cut out the template.

3 Place the template on the cushion approximately 2in (5cm) away from an edge and trace using a pencil. Then flip the template over to create a mirror image and trace again next to the first flower.

4 With the flowers traced, open the cushion cover and place the inner ring inside the cushion. Place the outer ring over the top on the outside and stretch the cushion in the hoop, so that the first flower is taut.

5 The fabric of the cushion will have relatively evenly spaced holes like monk's cloth, however they will be a little closer together. Make sure to push your punch needle between the gaps in the weave, all the way down to the handle when you punch.

6 Thread your punch needle in the first colour and start punching the outline of the flower. Aim for small stitches and try to punch in each hole or space where you can. Once you have punched the first flower, move the hoop over to re-tighten and punch the second flower.

7 When you have punched both of the flower outlines on the outside (right side) of the cushion, turn the cushion inside out.

8 Re-stretch the first flower head in your hoop.

9 Inside the flower head at the base of the flower, punch a small circle (it is punched using yellow yarn here, but choose a colour you like). Punch in every hole or space where possible, starting with the outline and then working your way into the centre.

10 Don't leave gaps in between your rows here, keep the stitches close together.

11 Snip your yarn when you reach the centre of the circle and push the end through to the front.

12 Repeat for the second flower.

13 When you have punched these circles, remove the cushion fabric from the hoop and turn the cushion back so the right side is facing outwards.

14 Trim the ends of your yarn so they are flush.

ABSTRACT WALL HANGING

The bold design used for this circular picture is strong enough to make a stand-alone statement feature on any wall in your home, or for a really unique feature wall make a collection to display – for added interest vary your placement of shades and express your creative self.

SKILL LEVEL: MOVING ON

YOU'LL NEED:

- 10in (25.5cm) embroidery hoop

- Monk's cloth fabric – 11¾in (30cm) square

- Approximately 200g of medium-weight yarn (CYC group 4)

- #14 Oxford fine punch needle

- Fabric scissors

- Embroidery scissors or snips

- Darning needle

- Tape measure

STATIONERY:

- Permanent marker or pencil

- PVA (or alternative strong glue) and fine paintbrush

ABSTRACT WALL HANGING

Size: The wall hanging will be made using a 10in (25.5cm) embroidery hoop and this will be the finished size.

ABOUT THE PROJECT

The flat stitches will be visible on the finished side of the hoop, with the outer hoop covered in yarn.

METHOD

To punch the wall hanging

Unlike some of the other projects where you will work in a frame or hoop, remove your project and finish it in another way, this wall hanging will be made in the embroidery hoop and then remain there for finishing.

1 Measure and cut an 11¾in (30cm) square piece of monk's cloth.

2 You do not need to do anything to secure the edges of the fabric, as you will be gluing it to the hoop.

3 Follow the instructions on pages 14–22 for more information on punching into an embroidery hoop, and how to stretch and glue your fabric into the hoop.

4 You will be punching on to the front of the hoop, so that the flat stitches are visible. They help to accentuate the angular nature of the design.

5 Once your fabric is stretched and glued into the hoop, trace the design on to the hoop. The template for the motif can be found on page 141 and needs to be copied at 138% (see page 14 for more information on how to effectively trace your design on to the fabric).

6 Thread your needle with your yarn and punch the different sections, start with the outline first and then fill in. You will want to keep your stitches as close as possible and ensure that all of the fabric is covered (see page 19 for more information on different stitches).

To finish the wall hanging

The outer edge of the embroidery hoop is covered using yarn and a whip-stitch. The lines of the design are carried on from the centre over the edge of the hoop. Following the instructions for whipping on page 25, cover the edge of the embroidery hoop with yarn.

7 When you have finished punching, turn over the hoop and snip off all of the ends flush with the loops.

8 As the flat stitches are visible on the front you will not need to do any tidying up of stitches.

TEMPLATES

Over the forthcoming pages you will find all the templates required for the projects. Use the tip for tracing the designs given on page 14. All templates are 100% unless otherwise stated.

SMALL GEOMETRIC CUSHION COVER (PAGE 26)
COPY AT 200%

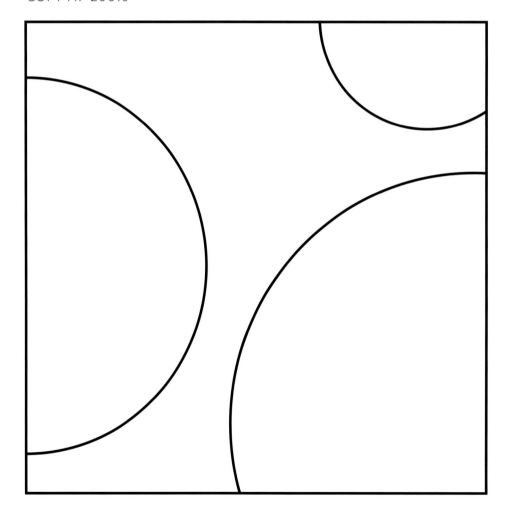

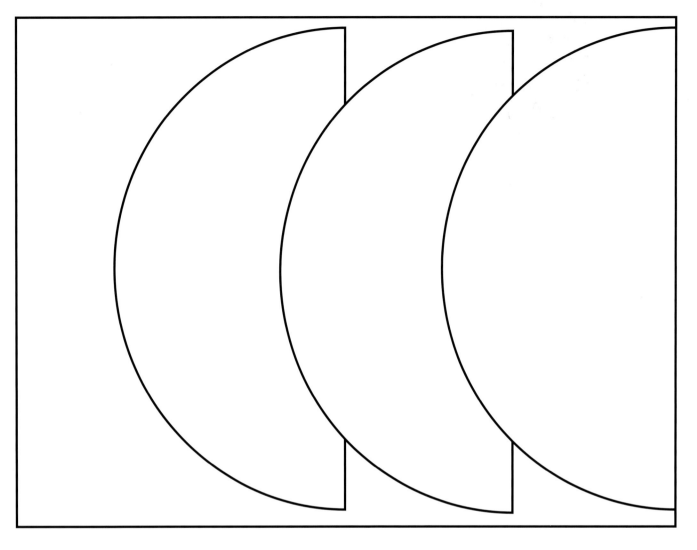

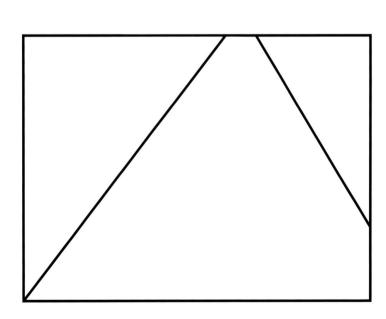

CARD HOLDER (PAGE 98)

TOOL TUB/LARGE STORAGE TUB (PAGE 38/42)

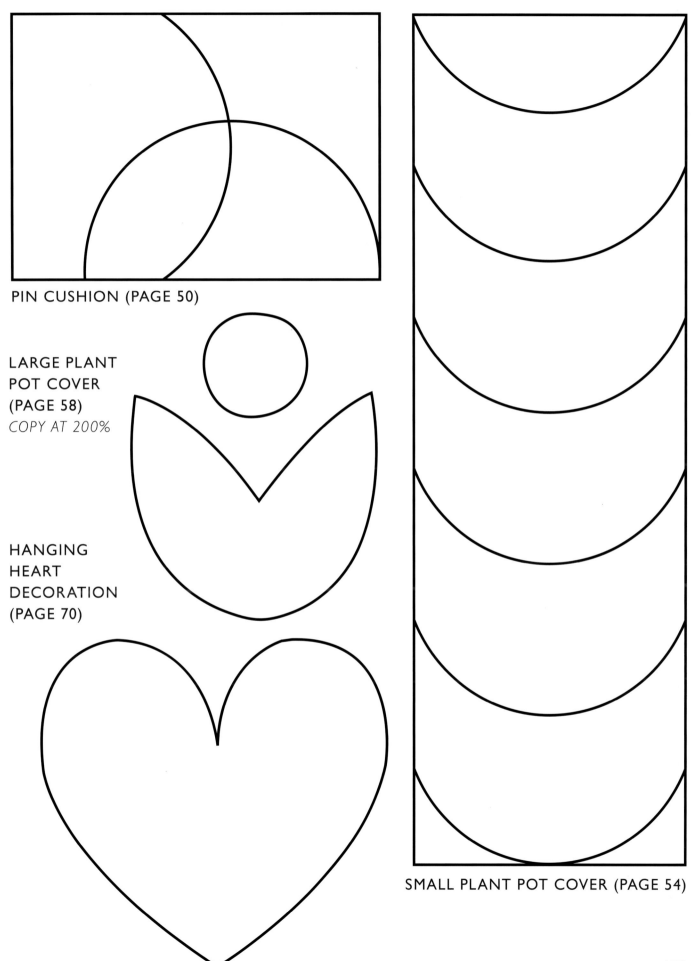

PIN CUSHION (PAGE 50)

LARGE PLANT
POT COVER
(PAGE 58)
COPY AT 200%

HANGING
HEART
DECORATION
(PAGE 70)

SMALL PLANT POT COVER (PAGE 54)

COASTERS (PAGE 74)

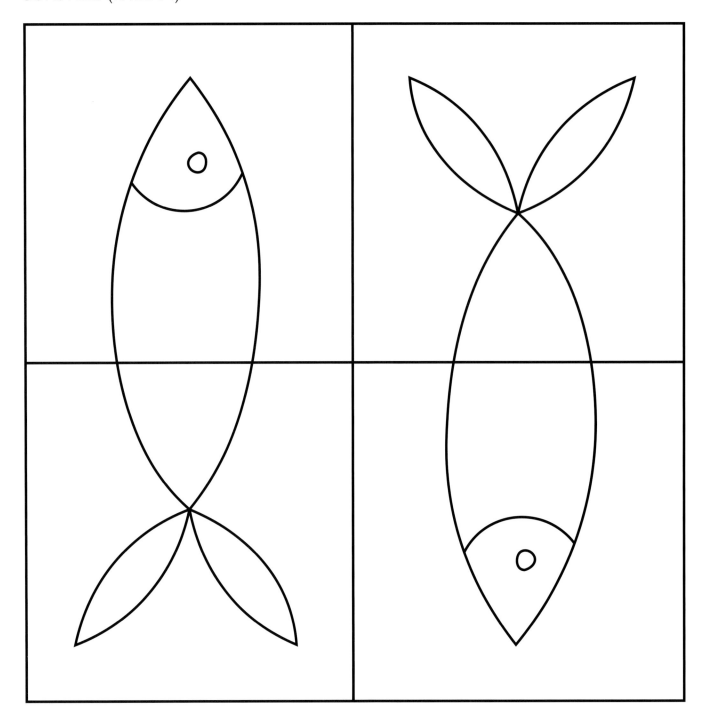

NAPKIN HOLDERS (PAGE 82)

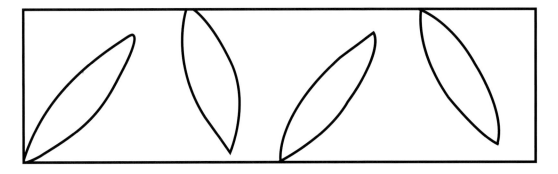

TRIVET (PAGE 78) *COPY AT 111%*

BOOKMARK (PAGE 86) *COPY AT 111%*

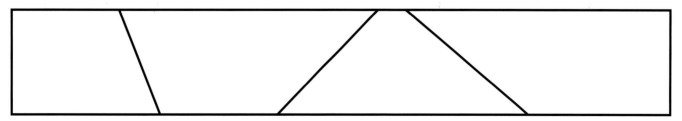

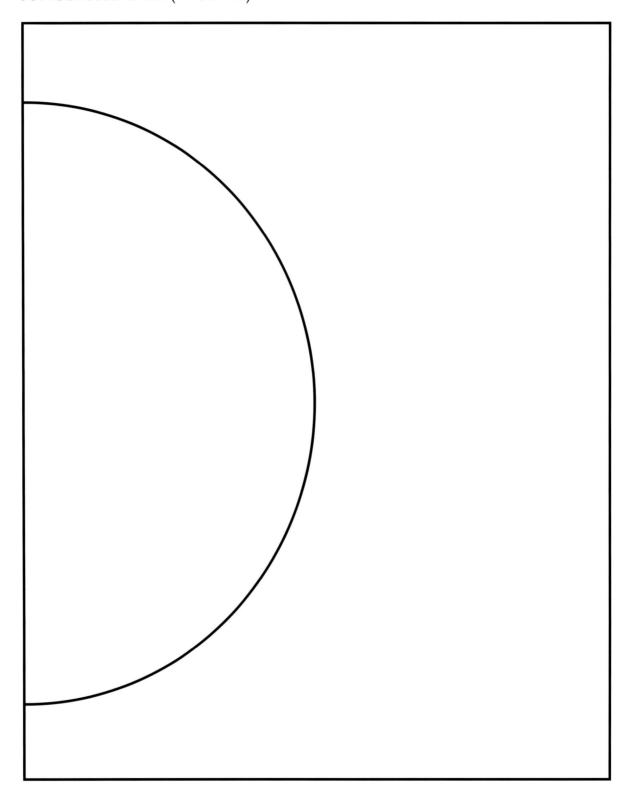

PASSPORT COVER (PAGE 106)

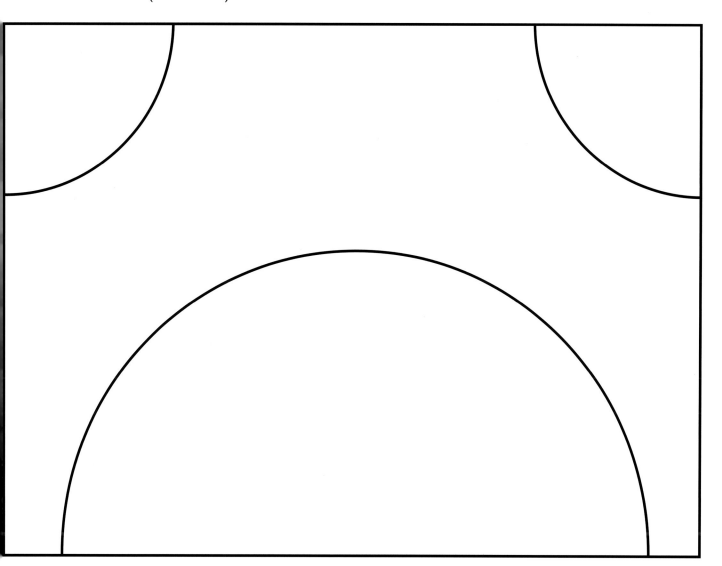

LAPTOP POUCH (PAGE 114) *COPY AT 200%*

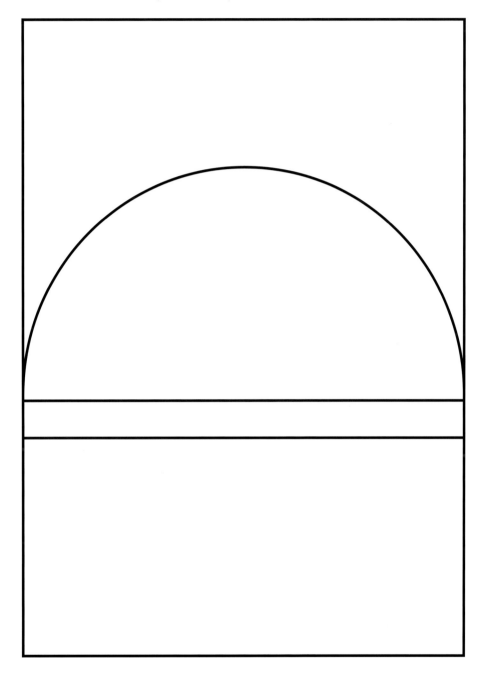

FRONT

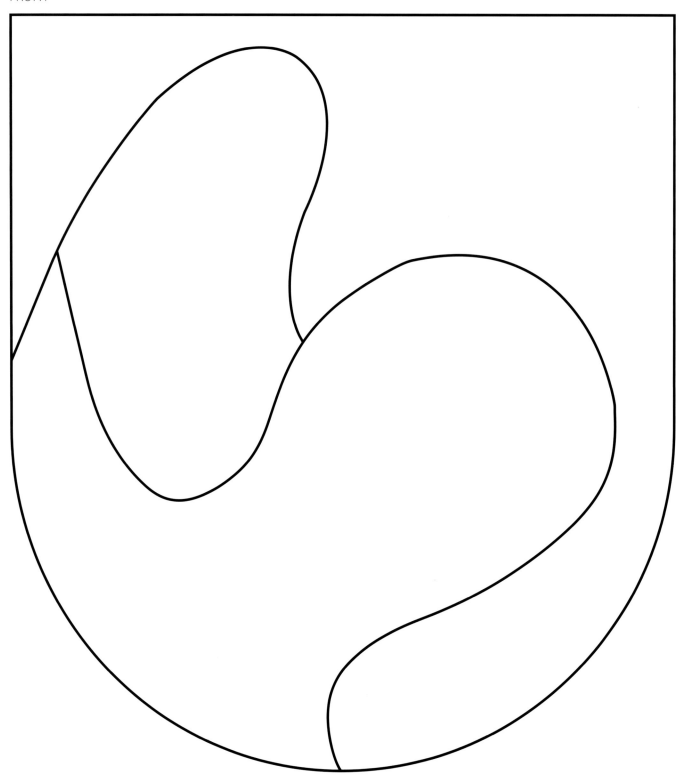

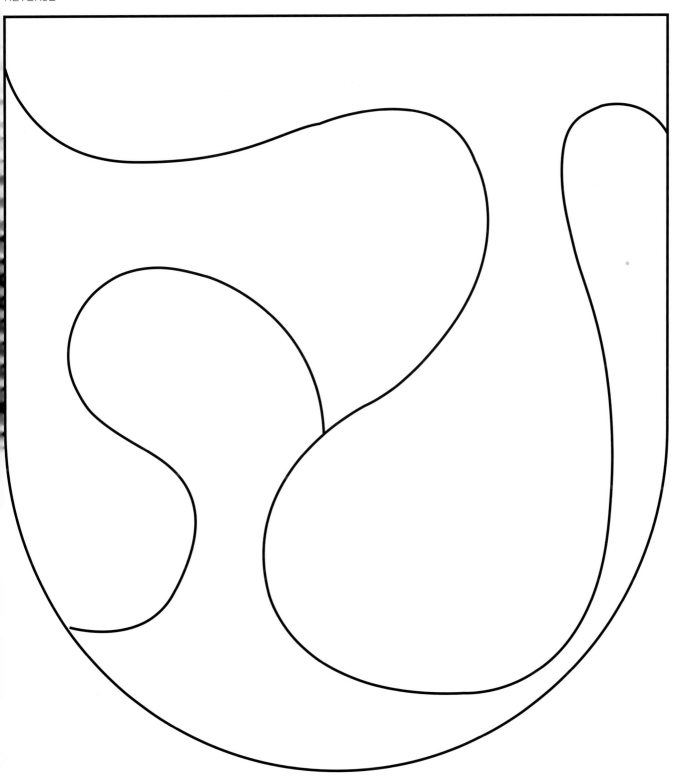

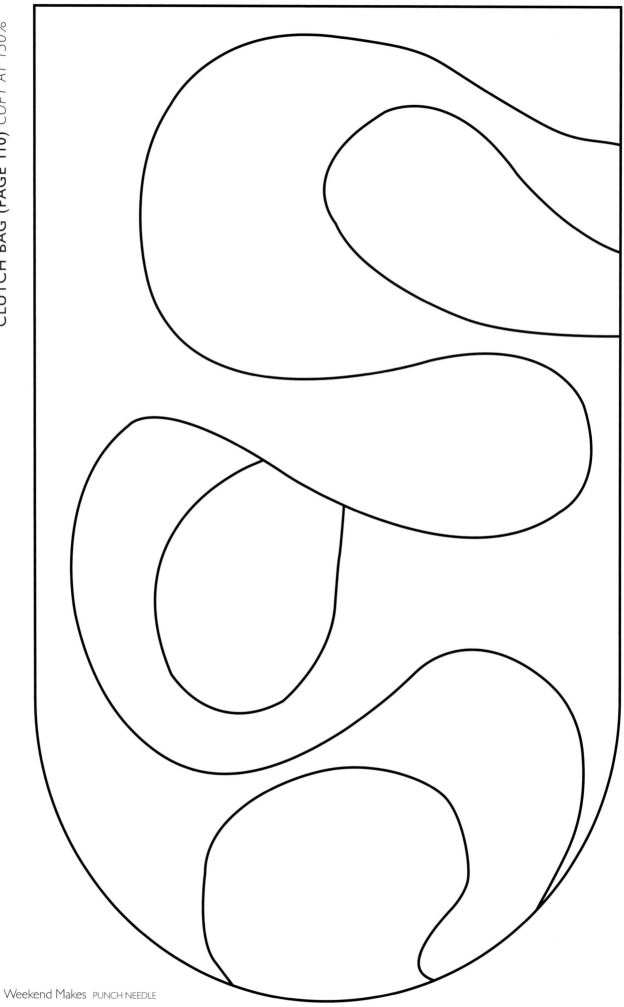

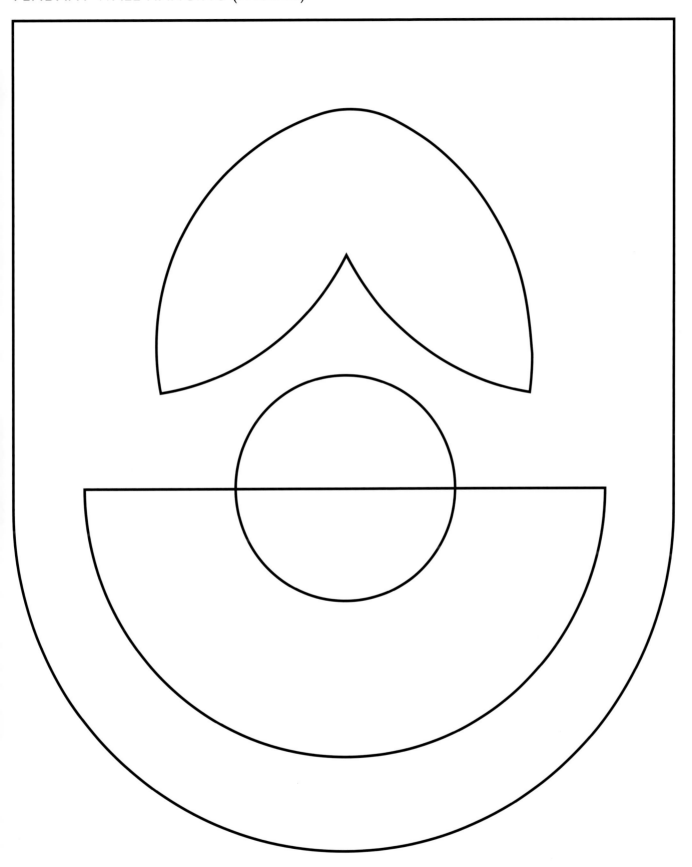

UPCYCLED CUSHION COVER (PAGE 118)

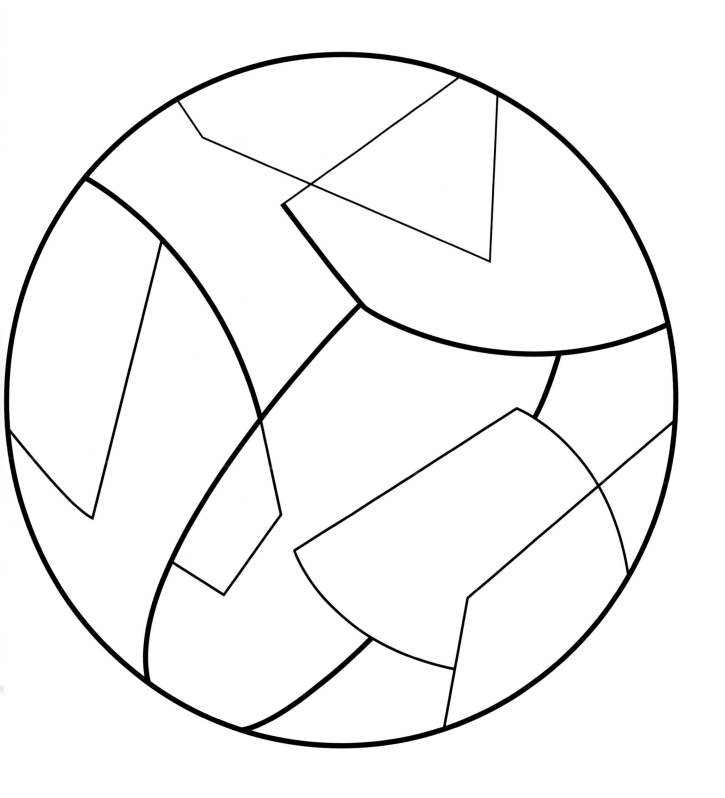

RESOURCES

Fabric
Monk's cloth – *wholepunching.co.uk*

Punch needles
Oxford punch needles – *wholepunching.co.uk*

Frames and hoops
No-slip hoops – *wholepunching.co.uk*
Canvas stretcher bars – *wholepunching.co.uk*
Gripper frames – *amyoxford.com*

Yarn
Medium, bulky and super bulky yarn
– *knitrowan.com*
Wool rug yarn – *wholepunching.co.uk*

Stationery, haberdashery and basic equipment
Hobbycraft – *hobbycraft.co.uk*

ACKNOWLEDGEMENTS

Thank you to everyone at Quail Studio for your guidance, support and for making writing my first book a thoroughly enjoyable experience.

To Amy, my mentor, forever an inspiration, your kindness astounds me. Thank you for creating an outstanding tool!

To my family, for your endless encouragement and unwavering enthusiasm in my endeavours.

Thank you to my partner Doug, for your continuous support and belief in me, I could not have done this without you.

Sara Moore

INDEX

A
Abstract Wall Hanging 122–125, 141

B
Bookmark 86–89, 131

C
Card Holder 98–101, 128
Celestial Hoop Art 90–93, 140
Clutch Bag 110–113, 138
Coasters 74–77, 130

D
Doorstop 62–65, 128
drawing a straight line 14

E
Equipment 12

F
fabric 9, 14
frames 10–11
frogging 21

G
Geometric Wall Art 46–49
gluing 23

H
Handbag 34–37, 136–137
Hanging Heart Decoration 70–73, 129
hemming 24
hoops 10–11, 16

L
Laptop Pouch 114–117, 135
Large Geometric Cushion Cover 30–33, 127
Large Plant Pot Cover 58–61, 129
Large Storage Tub 42–45, 128

N
Napkin Holders 82–85, 130

P
Passport Cover 106–109, 133
Pendant Wall Hanging 66–69, 139
Pin Cushion 50–53, 129
punch needle(s) 8, 16–20

S
Small Geometric Cushion Cover 26–29, 126
Small Plant Pot Cover 54–57, 129
steaming 23
stitches 19–20
stretching 15
Sunglasses Case 102–105, 132

T
Tablet Cover 94–97, 134
templates 126–141
Tool Tub 38–41, 128
tracing a pattern 14
Trivet 78–81, 131

U
Upcycled Cushion Cover 118–121, 140

W
whipping 25

Y
yarn 11

To order a book, or to request
a catalogue, contact:

GMC Publications Ltd
Castle Place, 166 High Street,
Lewes, East Sussex,
BN7 IXU
United Kingdom
Tel: +44 (0)1273 488005
www.gmcbooks.com